Children of the Shore

Children of the Shore

Growing up in Dingle in the 1950s and 1960s

John O'Connor

GARRAÍ PUBLICATIONS

GARRAÍ PUBLICATIONS
Dingle, Co Kerry, Ireland

A catalogue record for this book is available from the British Library.

ISBN 978-1-5272-6060-3

Editorial and publishing services by RED HEN PUBLISHING
www.redhenpublishing.ie

Typesetting and design by CARRIGBOY
www.carrigboy.com

Printed and bound in Spain by GRAPHYCEMS

For the descendants of Michael and Joan,
one hundred souls ... and counting

Contents

• • ● • •

Acknowledgements

····●····

I thank family members who encouraged this work and who helped with their recollections of times past in our house and in Dingle town. My brothers and sisters have kindly provided photographs which appear here – photographs which greatly enhance the appeal of this book and will lend themselves to many reminiscences of times past.

I wish to thank Noel Brosnan who provided valuable information regarding my ancestors from the Garraí in Dingle, and also for filling me in on aspects of life in Dingle in the early 1950s.

Thanks also to Bridget McAuliffe of Red Hen Publishing for her advice and guidance during the production of this book.

Introduction

·· ● ··

Dingle as I describe it here is no more. No inhabited place can be expected to stay the same after the passing of half a century. Cities and small towns the world over are vastly different places from what they were in the mid-20th century. Physical change is inevitable, but every city and small town has a character, a root that binds its inhabitant to it that can last a lifetime. Is the character of Dingle the same as it was when I was young? In the main, yes. People and community give a town its character, not buildings or enterprise, or trappings of popularity and fame.

In looking back, there is, naturally, an inclination by the chronicler to be influenced by nostalgia. And while the descriptions of events, places and things described here are from my lens, as it were, I am sure these descriptions will bring back memories of the time for many. There are bound to be differences in perspective; perspective, in such instances, encompasses not only visual absorption of the time in question, but state of mind as well. For example, a hungry and cold person will be distracted from the finer points of scenery and will disengage from the wonders of the place in which they live.

Dingle has, more than most towns, enjoyed success as a tourist destination, and has become quite cosmopolitan. Tourism began in earnest after the release of the West Kerry-made *Ryan's Daughter* in 1969. Though lame in plot, the film portrayed the magnificent scenery of the peninsula. The town was awash with famous actors – Mitchum, Mills, Miles, et al. But the cast of the David Lean-directed film were not the first Hollywood luminaries to visit the area; in 1968, Hollywood legend Gregory Peck and his family visited his Ashe cousins in Dingle, giving the small town in the back of beyond a connection with Hollywood. Nowadays, the place boasts visits from the likes of Tom Cruise, Ben Kingsley, Julia Roberts and a raft of others. We, locals, hardly give them a second glance but in the midst of such high-profile goings-on it would be hard for any town to remain unchanged.

There are now two principal seasons in Dingle: the tourist season and the other, with the former extending from its traditional three-month period to half the year. The tourist business is, as they say, 'good for the town'. The omnipresent tourist dollar is now king and the attendant reverence administered to the visitor is evident and understandable.

Yet, in spite of this acquired status as a town that draws profitable footfall, there remains, though in some cases hidden, a flavour of the town's true character which is still recognised by many families who have emigrated and return from time to time.

In looking back, nostalgia will always be a factor as we long for the things that have gone, and any assessment we make, from today's viewpoint, will be influenced by our romanticising of the past. Yet, the times we lived in are only accurately assessed from a distant viewpoint. While in the throes of being reared in testing times and trying to make a living, there is little inclination for analysing one's surroundings and the meaning of life – that is a luxury for idle minds and for people who know where their next meal is coming from.

. • .

Several of our stomping grounds have vanished down through the years. The gas shed at the head of the pier where fishermen whiled away the bad days as they waited for the weather to change gave way recently to a tourist office – an apt example of the new priorities of the Quay area and the town. The indigenous fishing industry in Dingle is negligible. The pier has now, in the main, become a landing place for foreign fishing boats whose produce is trucked out of town. The port in general accrues much of its income from the leisure industry – tourist ferry boats and visiting yachtsmen. Dingle Boatyard, which was turning out fine fishing boats for more than forty years, is long gone. The site is now a vacant lot and awaits development. The skills of the men who crafted the vessels lie dormant and, in another generation, will be gone forever.

The old Dingle Hospital, in whose walls much of the town's history is steeped, is boarded up; the replacement facility is a very welcome addition to the town. Dingle Technical School was demolished following a restructuring of second-level education in the area and has been replaced by Dingle Oceanworld, a successful tourism enterprise. The Christian Brothers School has found a new use as an international off-campus facility for an American college.

While we have lost a lot since the days of our youth, there have been gains. These stemmed mainly from the making of the aforementioned *Ryan's Daughter* and the arrival of the Dingle Dolphin, Fungie, in the early 1980s. But back as far as 1936, Dingle's potential as a tourist destination had been spotted. That year, the Irish Tourist Association produced a filmed travelogue, entitled *The Irish Riviera*, which featured the southwest coast of Ireland. The Dingle Peninsula was included, with scenes of Dingle, Ballydavid and Dunquin showcasing the area at the time.

We now live in a popular tourist town and enjoy the benefits that go with that. However, whereas the quality of life has improved for many, for others it has deteriorated. Due to the influx of large numbers of people during the visitor season, the simple, everyday act of walking the streets has become an onerous navigational chore rather than the heretofore leisurely saunter. Locals are scarce on the cluttered paths, waiting to emerge again when a respite from the heavy footfall comes around in the months with an 'r' in them. Green fields have disappeared and hillsides are dotted with holiday homes. Some of our traditional local celebrations, such as that on New Year's Eve, have been appropriated by strangers for *their* amusement. We are beset by the double-edged sword of fame.

People say, 'You knew everybody in town in the old days'. Perhaps this is so; perhaps it is a meaningless, throwaway remark, or an expression of a desire for kinship. No doubt, a sense of belonging is important within family and community. People don't want to be left out. To that end, Dingle people, especially those with roots in the town, should feel comfortable with the new direction of *their town* and feel that they, by dint of their heritage, are still valued.

Nobody, from a poor family at any rate, wants to go back to the 1950s and 1960s and experience again the hard times that were endured. It is a fact of life that adversity engenders invention and a will to rise above and do better. A dose of hardship (though ours was prolonged and became a way of life) will do more to form character and instil drive than serene living.

This book has at its root a family growing up in hard times in the Dingle of the 1950s and 1960s; a family that were not alone in their struggle in a town that had several poor neighbourhoods. Dingle, being largely dependent on the fishing industry as an employer, had several fisherman families and, due to the inconsistency of the industry, many families were in want for long periods and lived in the barest of accommodation. However, families struggled on, scrimping and providing as best they could. In those decades, the expectations of, and opportunities for, families on the poverty line for moving forward were negligible. It was a period that dragged out for what seemed like forever before possibilities for the future finally started to emerge.

ONE

House and Neighbourhood

·· ● ··

I still live in the house I was born in. Not many people my age can say that. Out of the twenty-two houses in my street, only two more people who grew up there have that distinction. I sometimes think of what it was like for my brothers and sisters to leave (I was gone intermittently from the house in the middle years) and wonder what it is like for them to now visit the house they were born in. Based on the frequency of their visits, it is evident that the house still has an attraction for them; there is a pull that seems to draw them back to the walls that sheltered them in their childhood. A house can develop a benign character, a pleasing aura, for people who were born and reared in that *homeplace*. It is also the case with an ancestral home, like our grandfather's in the Garraí which is still available for us to visit. There is a vibe there; a contentment in knowing that this is where you came from.

The stone walls of our house were solid. They enveloped us in the cocoon of our birth and youth and, if they could talk, they would tell much more than I am prepared to reveal here. I am constrained by judiciousness and, while harbouring a desire to be fair and true, I am prepared to leave behind some of the more intimate, and perhaps more revelatory, happenings to the walls that were privy to the joys and difficulties of the twelve who brushed against their soft-plastered interior.

The physical walls bounded us from the outside world while, within, less visible boundaries helped maintain order in the inevitable chaotic assembly of such a large number of occupants in the confined space. Having one's own space was a concept not imagined by dwellers in low-income houses. In the 1950s, having a roof over their children's heads was the principal aim of parents, and their resolve to achieve that aim was often hampered by the uncertainty of the times which produced generations of poor and desperate people who lived from day to day with no plans for an always uncertain future. There were a number of indigent neighbourhoods in the town, all sharing in common the need for more food, clothing, money, respect, and the wish for certainty about the future as each day brought more of the same drudgery.

We had some luck on our side, though. Our house passed on to my father from his uncle who had lived in it until his death in the mid-1940s. The building was one of fifteen built by the county council in 1909 to house fishermen and their families and some general workers. Solidly built of stone and roofed with natural slate of substantial thickness, they must have looked grand at the start of the century. My father, Michael, moved in after he got married in 1947.

The Cottages, as they came to be known, were approaching their fiftieth year when I was nine, and looking their age due to lack of maintenance. The original joinery of doors and windows, still intact though shrunken, provided pathways for the shrieking cold air of winter which rattled a whistling dance to the howling winds. My father would stuff newspaper into the gaps between the sashes to hold at bay the incessant invasion of draughts which robbed the home of any heat that existed within. By that time, too, the plaster render under the slates had started crumbling, and this opened up scores more cracks to the elements beyond. The dust from the plaster would make its way between the ceiling boards and down onto the beds during windy nights.

· • ·

My father's lineage goes back to a hamlet called Reenbeg, on the southern shore of Dingle Harbour, where his grand-mother, and my great-grandmother, Elizabeth Ashe lived. Elizabeth moved across the harbour to Dingle and married Jeremiah O'Connor from Quay Street (now Strand Street) in 1862. Elizabeth and Jeremiah had nine children, one being my grandfather James. James married Mary Deady and set up home in the Garraí (small garden), a laneway branching off from Strand Street at the Quay.

Mikey Connor, as my father was known, was born into a whitewashed cottage in the Garraí, where the family was sustained by fishing. Most of the residents from the Quay and laneways that branched off it were of fishing stock.

My father was from a family of eight. Mary Deady was a holy woman and would follow her husband – and my father in later years – down the laneway at five o'clock in the morning, sprinkling holy water over them as they departed for the fishing grounds.

My mother, Joan, hailed from a small holding in north Kerry near Dirha, Listowel. Her father, Jack Brennan, and his wife, Mary (née Buckley), worked a small farm and had four more offspring. As children, we never got to know our mother's people to any great degree, distance and travel being a factor in those days. I have memories of my grandmother, dressed in black and wearing a shawl, coming to Dingle on the odd occasion, bringing a message bag full of much-needed goodies. I visited the farm in Dirha a couple of times when very young; my main recollection of one visit is of me breaking the handle of the mangle pulper.

Joan came to Dingle to work as a housekeeper (to the Garvey household in the mid-1940s), and that move left one less mouth to feed on the small north Kerry farm. Our mother would often tell us how she and our father used to meet in the Phoenix Ballroom in Dingle on Saturday nights; she, dressed in her finery, and our father coming in tipsy and making a beeline for her. It sounded like romantic, innocent and carefree times. Then came marriage, followed by children and more children and the daily struggle to keep the wolf from the door.

· • ·

Our beginnings, in 122, The Wood, were humble and rudimentary. They were beginnings from whence five boys and five girls sprung into a household and a world where they would find love, hate, class distinction, poverty, hypocrisy and, in later years, hope. The easier days for my parents were surely those when the numbers were small and Mary, Nuala and I were all they had to feed and clothe. My earliest memory of home is when I was four, having a birthday party with Angela, who was next to me on the younger side, and the two older girls around the table. We did have birthday parties in spite of the other wants in the household.

Mary was born in the year of a big storm. Nuala was born on St Stephen's Day to the sound of the Wrenboys passing the door, and claims she can remember the music of the fifes and drums. I was the third in line, born in February, a Piscean. As the family multiplied, the pressures mounted. Before the mid-1950s, Michael and Carmel arrived and after that, up to 1962, the arrival of Bernadette, Ignatius, Anthony, and Ambrose completed the ten who would need sustenance in number 122.

The nuns of the local Presentation Convent are credited with naming some of the later children to arrive in the house. We were born in a time when children were named after saints, rather than soap stars. The first five children were born at home and the remaining five in the local hospital. Before taking to the bed to have the child, our mother would get down on her knees and scrub the floor of the big room, which was the upstairs bedroom, while a local midwife would assist with the birth. Apart from all the other daily demands of running a home, having nappies washed and dried was a huge task for our mother. I remember the clothesline with the square shapes of laundered white cloth billowing in the wind. When the weather was foul, they would be stacked on the metal bars above the range.

A metal bath was placed in the middle of the floor on Saturday nights and filled with hot water. Lifebuoy soap was added and the children squabbled as to who got in first. Our toilet was a lean-to accessed through the yard and it had squares of newspaper hanging on a hook. In those days, the sewage was piped directly into the harbour where, despite that, cockles, mussels and periwinkles thrived. In later years, when the grandchildren from the house visited, they would run through the backyard to the sea wall after flushing the toilet and lean over it to see their deposit exiting the pipe. What fun! For night-time calls of nature, there were white enamel poo pots (with lids) in the bedrooms.

· • ·

The big bedroom upstairs accommodated the growing family in the early years; an adjacent smaller room (supposed to be haunted), housing miscellaneous junk, was not used until much later when the older children were in their early teens. The youngest child slept downstairs with our parents in the third bedroom until of age to graduate to a cot manufactured from a wooden fish box by my father and situated upstairs in the big room. The child in the box would be shielded from the wooden splinters by any spare apparel found idle.

The beds in the big room were of the spring-base variety (and probably there since the house was built). On top of them were lumpy mattresses with peaks and troughs like a distressed cross-sea. All four rooms in the house had fireplaces, but it was rare to have the ones upstairs lit for reasons of safety and due to scarcity of firewood.

When we were all gathered upstairs for the night, there would be shenanigans which generated laughter and commotion which led to loud recriminations from below stairs. Our mother would shout warnings, threatening withdrawal of privileges for the offenders. Privileges, indeed! What could be taken from us? We had nothing of worth but our comradery. Joan would sometimes sneak up the stairs in the hope of naming the culprit but a shrunken, creaking step would give us forewarning of her intent.

In summer, we would sometimes stay awake through the night and get up at dawn to start exploring in the strand and beyond. Anyone who fell asleep during the agreed vigil was remonstrated with for not playing the game. It was in the big room that the essence of our group was formed. The childish games and carry-on which mostly embraced laughter and frivolity was, unknown to us, forming a foundation on which a meaningful, cohesive unit was being built. It is still the room where all of the family want to sleep when they visit the family home.

My first memory of the small room upstairs being used was when a mysterious man named Scanlon visited our house. This man was reputed to be a cousin of our mother and he had cycled from Tipperary to spend a number of weeks with us. His provenance was unclear to us – and still is – and I remember my father shaking his head in wonderment at the man having cycled from distant Tipperary … it's a long way to Tipperary and all that! However, a mattress was laid on the floor of the small room for the energetic tourist and he duly resided and shared at our table whose bounty was already under pressure from a hungry horde.

· • ·

The fourth room (the main downstairs room) was where we lived during the day and was, in every respect, where we *lived*. It was our kitchen and living room, our parlour and our sitting room; it was where we hung out and generally came in the way of our mother as she went about the business of rearing us. In those days, the admonishing order from a parent to 'Go to your room' would not have been heard, and one could not go to their room and sulk over some falling out. One had to grin and bear any real or imagined infraction in the same space as one's accuser – a small squabble could turn into uproar as each side of the argument gained support from the sidelines.

There were the inevitable rivalries amongst the siblings. Being the oldest boy, I was challenged regularly by Michael, the next in the male line, for my place in the pecking order. Anthony and Ambrose, the two youngest, had at it hammer and tongs mainly because Ambrose, the last born and known as the 'baby' well into his older years, was the favoured pet of our mother. Ignatius, who was in the middle, got grief from both camps; this encouraged him to gain independence and shy away from the political rivalries of his brothers.

The girls had their own brand of mayhem. Hair-pulling and name-calling occurred regularly with the younger ones. Mary and Nuala, being the oldest two, were minders when the younger ones came along. Angela, in the middle of the girls, ploughed her own furrow. The whole daytime drama of the house played out in the living room where all were present. The children bore witness to our parents' disagreements, which caused considerable commotion at times. Before soap opera came into our homes via television, we had the genuine article in the living room at 122, The Wood.

. • .

The living room contained the stairs and a small scullery beside the back door which led to an old, damp and cold shed where coal and various discarded items were stored. There was an old dresser, painted a light-blue colour, beside the dining table which was in the corner beside the western front window. The kitchen table and various fitments close by were painted in the same shade of blue, as were the mud guards on our father's bike and the lower half of the exterior front wall of the house. Paint wasn't wasted, and any left over from first usage was employed ad infinitum until the can was emptied. Several cottages were painted using an array of colours which didn't adhere to any concept of colour schemes as we know them now. The other predominant colour in our lives was pink, which was found on most of the interior walls. We lived in a world of basic colours.

Two painted benches were situated on each side of the table. A seat modified from a wooden barrel was cornered on the left of the fireplace, which was a metal range in poor repair. That said, it was the only source of heating for the house and we were to be found huddled around it in winter, all trying to get as close as possible to its warm glow. At night, for a treat, we toasted bread skewered on a poker over the flame. The range was our cooker as well, and was complemented by a primus which boiled water, mainly for tea. It wasn't until the later 1960s that a gas cooker arrived at 122.

A rickety armchair was placed to the right of the range. This is where my father would sit at night-time to read and relax after his day, in so far as relaxation could be found amid the chaos of the household. Our father would, in calmer moments in the house, play the tin whistle or the harmonica to entertain us; he always encouraged participation in singing and music. The lower steps of the stairs provided seating when high occupancy demanded it. The space beneath the stairs was used for storage. We didn't have a fridge until I was in my late teens. I remember being embarrassed bringing friends to the house because we didn't have a place to keep the milk from souring; a fridge, in any event, would have been redundant in the early years.

The first radio that I remember had heavy, rechargeable batteries. This was followed by a more modern type – a Bush which required disposable batteries. When we first got it, my mother would play it loud and open the front door so the neighbours could hear the music and deduce that we, at least, had a radio in the house. Our mother was proud that way, eager to show off and display that the household was not entirely destitute. One of the first advertising jingles I remember from the radio was for toothpaste: *You'll wonder where the yellow went when you brush your teeth with Pepsodent*. We grew up without television, which finally came to our house in the 1970s.

The bottom presses of the old dresser were off limits to the children. The valuables held there, meagre as they were, had personal and sentimental value for Michael and Joan. In later years, our mother would hide the newspaper there, too; she always wanted to be first with the news. On the doors of the dresser, a brass fitting with a ring-pull held a fascination for the younger children who would jangle it to hear its ringing sound. That ringing sound is still in the house; the fitting now on a new internal door.

A couple of wooden tea chests were situated in corners. They were used to store clothes, bedding, and other odds and ends. Our parents' bedroom was off limits unless we were expressly summoned to its quarters. In later years, when the family had thinned out after some had left home, the downstairs bedroom became a sitting room, complete with flowery wallpaper put up by our father.

There was a sizeable backyard where rubbish, firewood and coal (when the going was good) was kept. In later years, my father sat potatoes in one quarter of the space. There was a holly tree and rose bushes bloomed in summer. Beyond the backyard, a laneway separated us from a formidable sea wall beyond which was our extended playground. We would spend our days in summer on the shore, skimming stones, turning over rocks and foraging for imagined treasure.

My father collected the seaweed for fertilising his potato ridges. He was also a beachcomber, often collecting items of dubious value which ended up in our backyard. Rusted pram wheels, biscuit tins and the odd headless doll were among the booty. Our mother would often throw items she deemed nonsensical back over the wall. At one time, our Dad brought back a single shoe from the strand and our Mom promptly got rid of it when he was not looking. Some days later, he came back from the strand with another shoe and proclaimed joyously that he had found the comrade of the previous one – it was the same shoe that our mother had discarded.

· • ·

A middle-aged brother and sister resided on the town side of our house. While playing with a ball in our backyard, the ball would frequently go over the neighbours' wall and getting permission to retrieve it from the woman in the house, who would get annoyed after numerous infractions, was something none of us wanted to do. To the immediate west of us, a single man, Edwin, lived alone until in later years when his brother, Jimmy, arrived out of nowhere.

Edwin was easy-going and had a peculiar turn of phrase when discussing anything; he tried to find a bit of fun in the most mundane things.

The boundary wall between us and Edwin was low and everything going on in both yards was open to all. I wonder now what it was like for Edwin to live beside a gang of noisy, unruly children. I fell off the wall into his garden when I was very young and landed in a bunch of nettles. The resultant agony, exacerbated by my wearing short pants, was my first introduction to prolonged physical discomfiture. Edwin was quick with a comforting tone and advice to find a dock leaf to ease the sting.

The Cottages consisted of fifteen houses divided into three blocks of five houses each. In our block, we were the only house with children. Further along, there was a childless couple who kept a neat house, and next to them lived an old lady whose voice reverberated along the block when she spoke. There were two more houses in the street that had young children; the rest had a mix of elderly couples and widows. A tailor and his wife lived with their grown-up family in a house that had the best polished range in the neighbourhood. Pádraig, one of the sons from the house, was the town sacristan for more than sixty years. He introduced several boys in the neighbourhood to the skill of bell-ringing in the church tower at Angelus time. Next to them was an old woman called Nano who used to sit on a chair in her hall with the door open to watch the world go by.

One house had been vacant for a time until it was leased by a family from Tipperary who introduced more young children to the street. When my parents moved to the Cottages there were already established families where many of the children had grown and emigrated, one being that of my godmother Helen whom I met for the second time, after thirty years, in upstate New York where she was driving a school bus.

While the children from the street interacted regularly through school and play, our parents' contact with the neighbours was predicated mainly by proximity. My mother and a woman from three doors down used to have regular disagreements and would fall out every other week. We would be regularly warned not to have anything to do with 'that woman'. As children we never understood the politics of the street and the strife brought about by adult one-upmanship. Our mother, being from north Kerry, may have, for a time, been looked on as an outsider by some of the historic house owners; cosmopolitanism had not come to the Dingle of the 1950s. In the main, the households had good and kind people who grappled with the times as best they could. While some of the residents were comfortably off by the standards of the day, the houses with young children didn't have much to spare, and ours was, without question, in the direst situation.

To the east of the Cottages, an assortment of five dwellings stood on the same side of the street. Two of these were detached, privately built houses while the remaining three were terraced. Minnie, an old woman, lived alone in the house nearest to our cottages. She could be seen sitting inside the window where, on the inner sill, she kept a threepenny bit stuffed under the base of a small statue of the Virgin Mary. Next to Minnie, a quiet, middle-aged couple resided in what appeared to be a modicum of wealth. Then there was Begley's, the only shop in the street. Bridgie and Eamon lived next to the shop. I used to do odd jobs for Bridgie and she always treated me decently. She liked a bit of gossip and would confide to me the latest goings-on in the town that aroused her interest, always with the proviso, 'Don't quote me, John'. I liked her, she made me laugh.

Then, at the far end of the street, at the beginning of the outskirts of the town, a family that originated in West Cork had set up home. The patriarch of that family, John, managed the local boatyard and would one day become my first boss. Across the street there was one dwelling where a well-off family – the Keanes – lived. They had the first telephone and first car on the street, and it was the house where many of us first used the telephone.

That was our street – a diverse hodgepodge of humanity living on the shore of the harbour in houses that have, in recent years, been turned into holiday homes. Less than a third of the present-day occupants have a history on the street. Edwin, like many other historic owners, would not recognise his house now. Nothing stays the same. The former council cottages on the shore of the harbour have become much-desired properties. The new owners who now live in The Wood reside where many lives were played out against a backdrop of poverty and uncertainty that were part of the reality of life in those times.

O'Connor family photo, 1963. **Front, L to R** - Anthony, Bernadette, Ignatius.
Middle, L to R - Angela, Carmel, Michael. **Back, L to R** - John, Mary, Nuala,
Joan, Ambrose, Michael.

Grandfather, James O'Connor.

Michael O'Connor, left; James, middle; Jeremiah, right; in the Garraí.

Grandmother, Mary Deady O'Connor.

Mike O'Connor, grand-uncle to author, with Eileen, aunt to author, and her daughter Patricia.

Michael O'Connor and sister Eileen in the backyard of 122 The Wood.

James O'Connor with daughter Eileen and son Michael.

Michael O'Connor, **left and right**, with brother Jimmy, **middle**, right photo; at the hill near Eask Tower.

Mary Deady O'Connor, **middle**, with daughters: Eileen - **2nd from right**, Elizabeth, **right**; Josie, **back, right**. And friends.

The Garraí laneway, Dingle, with the Bowler brothers beside the O'Connor family home. Ita Brosnan is crossing the lane.

Michael and Joan Brennan O'Connor, wedding 1947.

John and Bernadette.

Mary O'Connor

Joan O'Connor and son Ambrose.

Michael O'Connor and son Anthony. Anthony, bottom.

O'Connor family in the sixties with visiting American cousins. **Back**: Michael, Joan, Bernadette, Carmel, John, Angela. **Front**: Michael, Ambrose, Vis., Anthony, Vis., Ignatius.

Michael and Joan O'Connor with Nicky Hawes - future son-in-law.

Boys at Dingle Regatta. Ciarán, Ignatius, John, Tommy.

Ignatius O'Connor.

TWO

Dingle in the 1950s and 1960s

·· ● ··

The sense of smell can trigger a memory quicker than any computer processor; the smell of burning furze on the hill, the sea air in autumn, freshly mown grass – these scents can transport you to a time, place or incident which had particular meaning. When I was growing up, the smell of fish along the quay was ever-present. Incense wafting from silver-jewelled urns in church ceremonies sparks memories of dominance and control by the clergy.

Sounds and visual imagery, like the Wren's Day, are also triggers that transport me to my younger days. The clip-clop of horses drawing carts was a familiar sound outside our door. Passing through Strand Street, the sounds of the boatyard were of mauls driving planks home to their frames with spikes. Caulking mallets striking irons that drove oakum into the plank seams provided an ongoing cacophony which we took for granted.

Along Holy Ground, a raft of tradesmen added their own din to the neighbourhood. The ding of hammer striking Tommy Barry's blacksmith's anvil could be heard from far off as we made our way to school. On the pier, the chug-chug of steamers and nobbies was a constant statement to the industry going on; this was also signalled by the wind-blown trail of exhaust smoke from the engines.

· • ·

On Saturday mornings, animals were driven past our house on the way to the fair field. We could hear the hubbub from our bedroom. Farmers and their workers, brandishing crooked blackthorn staffs, herded the animals along the streets after sunrise with a well-practised method. A sheepdog, under instruction from the herder, would scout ahead and stand guard at any openings in the road where the animals might stray. The street outside our house would be plastered with mushed cow pies, and the round droppings of sheep rolled freely in the midst of the footfall of cloven hooves. I used to help Andrew Landers, a friend of my father, to bring the animals to town. An added bonus to my participation was staying overnight in Landers' house the night before the drive and getting a chance to ride the resident white horse around the farm.

As the fair day got under way, there was a sense of something eventful and worthwhile happening in the town. While it was primarily a gathering for commercial benefit, it brought with it the attendant convivial atmosphere which emanates when some profit-making is in the offing. Balladeers selling song lyrics for a penny – or tuppence for a pamphlet – would weave their way through the crowds on the street. Songs by Percy French and traditional ballads of ancient origin were on offer. The shops and pubs made the most of the day and this beneficial gain trickled down the way, in some measure, to the workers.

In the evening, a song or two would be heard through the open doors of the drinking houses along Spa Road, which was closest to the fair field. As the day continued, the merriment would branch out to John Street and Main Street. Outside the pubs, horses would be tied to lamp posts awaiting their masters for the return trek to the east and west. There's a story about a farmer who, on arriving in town, tied his donkey and cart to a ladder which had a painter aloft, painting the pub wall.

The horse and cart was the main mode of transport for people and goods. On the way to school, I would see carts in various stages of construction by wheelwrights along the Holy Ground where several craftsmen, including two shipwrights, two wheelwrights, a carpenter and a blacksmith, resided, all next door to each other. When the wooden wheels were ready, the blacksmith would build a fire around a steel band and heat the rim until it was red hot. He would then lift it onto the wheel with tongs and douse it with water from the Mall River. The expanded rim would sizzle and release a fog into the air as it cooled and contracted, driving the spokes home to felloes and hub – physics at play as passers-by walked nonchalantly past.

The horse and cart gradually gave way to mechanised vehicles. At local level, the tractor was making inroads and lorries were becoming a regular appearance on the roads, which were gradually improving in quality. One such lorry that came to town once a week was coloured green and had GEARY'S printed in large letters on it; in local lore this lorry was always a harbinger of bad weather.

· • ·

Walking through the town back then, we saw stuff we will never see again. That is the way of generational change. We all think that the change we went through was the most significant. What puts this in perspective for me, in one respect, is the memory of the town crier, Old (Jim) Cronesberry. I remember him marching through the streets, ringing a bell, as he announced forthcoming events and gatherings – circuses coming to town, news of the arrival of steamers (steam ships which brought goods, mostly coal and grain in my time, for local merchants), and such like. Sometime later, posters started appearing in shop windows and some news started to be passed down the lines of the telephone. A telegram came to our house to let us know our grandmother in Listowel had died.

In the 1960s, some members of the family had pen pals, who were to be found in the pages of magazines. I found a bottle in the strand with a message from a German merchant seaman named Michael Titz. The bottle had been thrown overboard in the mid-Atlantic and had made its way to the shoreline at the back of our house. There was much excitement in number 122 because any occurrence that might involve a possible prize or financial reward was very welcome. The seaman and I corresponded for a time, and I had imaginings of having found a benefactor.

The drawn-out process of writing letters back then and waiting for the reply had elements of suspense and anticipation. The order of the day by female correspondents, my sisters included, especially if they were writing to a potential paramour, was to sign off the letter with the acronym SWALK (sealed with a loving kiss). Nowadays, there is instant communication worldwide through ever-growing media platforms. In the course of half a century, I have spanned a communication age from Old Cronesberry, town crier, to Mark Zuckerberg, social media tycoon.

· • ·

The architecture of the streets and laneways was a mix of well-to-do solid stone houses with natural slate on pitched roofs, and white-washed cottages with tarred felt roof coverings, like the house my father was born in. The layout of the O'Connor house in the Garraí where he was born, with an open loft where children slept, was common to the times in poorer neighbourhoods. Similar dwellings lined many of the laneways that branched out from the main streets. In the Garraí and Colony, half-doors were left open throughout the day and women wearing black shawls would bend over them and talk hither and tither to their counterparts across the narrow divide of the dirt street. This region was known as the Quay and it extended from the Cottages (in The Wood) to include Strand Street. Rambunctious young males from the area were known as the 'Quay fellas'.

The Garraí had a well at the top end which supplied the water needs of my ancestors and their neighbours. The Colony had its own well and a suction-type water pump was later sited at the lower end of the street. Later again, this was replaced by a modern mains supply. Similar pumps were located at strategic intersections around the town. Along the main streets, three-storey-high cast-iron sewer vents rose into the air. The gas shed (which originally stored gas for the lamps on the pier) at the head of the pier was a hangout for my father and my Uncle Jerry. There, groups of fishermen would meet and moan about the bad weather and talk about the state of the fishing and all other ailments pertaining to the harbour and its environs, and the world at large.

• • •

Dingle is famously known as having had fifty-two pubs back in the day. Many were small and several had dual and triple functions, which included drapery, general merchant and serving as a small household shop. Several had snugs, some of which still exist, as in Curran's and Dick Mack's. Historically, snugs segregated women from the male-dominated main bar, where manly discussion prevailed. The tables have turned in that respect – the men are now in the snugs while women drinkers hold court on the main floor. In the 1970s, when tourism was taking hold, many of the pubs tore out the old-fashioned woodwork fixings and, in some cases, the adjacent living room, and made way for shiny, modern-looking drinking emporiums.

There were three tailors in the town, along with two barbers and about two dozen woodwork craftsmen, between carpenters, wheelwrights and shipwrights. There were also bakers, blacksmiths, harness makers, painters and half a dozen shoemakers who served a population whose needs were, in the main, simple.

The largest working group, apart from farmers, were the fishermen. The fleet consisted of twenty-plus boats, with each having an average crew of four. Fishing provided incomes for upwards of eighty families when the weather allowed. My grandfather fished in a sailing 'nobby' – a fishing boat introduced to Ireland from the Isle of Mann in 1890. My father and his brother Jeremiah also donned the yellow oilskins required for spending long hours in all kinds of weather trawling in Dingle Bay.

The onshore benefits of the fishing industry were visible along the seafront where a number of stalls selling the day's catch were situated. The pubs along the Quay did well when the going was good, as did the shops and the aforementioned tradesmen; the ripple effect of the economy is not a new thing. When I was four, the newly operational Bord Iascaigh Mhara (BIM) boatyard launched its first fishing trawler. A series of fifty-foot, black-hulled vessels were completed in the early years before taking on larger boats. As the number of workers increased, the yard produced two vessels a year. The boatyard was the first significant craft industry in Dingle at the turn of the mid-century mark. It became a valuable employer and trainer of skilled craftsmen and was also where I trained as a shipwright and got my first permanent job. My first week's wages, issued by BIM, were £3, fifteen shillings and eleven pence, a sizeable amount for a sixteen-year-old at the time.

· • ·

Our family members passed the Quay every day of their young lives. Going to school, at work or at play, it was central to our existence outside the house. It was a hub of activity where the commerce of the fishing industry played out. In my father's youth, fleets of nobby fishing boats would land their catch at the sandstone pier. In my grandfather's time, a hundred nobbies – several of them visiting and landing their catch – were often berthed on the east side of the pier. This rafting of boats enabled a fisherman to step off the pier onto a boat and hop from vessel to vessel as far as the Cooleen shore on the far side. That congestion of boats had receded by my time, though a sizeable fleet still existed. The nobbies were eventually replaced by the fifty-footers.

One of my earliest memories of the pier is of a local boat bringing the remains of battered currachs to the pier after tragedy had befallen them and their crews while fishing for mackerel west along the peninsula. I was nine at the time and under the wing of my father and Uncle Jerry as the crowd gathered by the quay-side to witness the solemn event.

The arrival of steamers (cargo ships) bringing coal and grain to Dingle gave opportunity for short-term employment while the ships were being unloaded. A regular troupe of wiry workers, which included my brother Michael when he was scarcely sixteen, would emerge from the holds in the evening, as dark as midnight from coal and slag dust.

Apart from the workers in the holds of the ship, several farmers were employed with their horses and carts drawing the cargo from the Quay to the yards of local merchants where scores more men were signed on to empty and store the loads from the carts. There were three rates of pay for the workers; on board, the steamer workers were paid per ton unloaded, the cart men were paid by the cartload delivered to the yard, and the yard workers were paid by the hour. The pubs along the Quay also got their bit out of the enterprise. My sisters Nuala and Mary were warned by our mother to be demure and plain while passing Sheehy's pub lest they be taken away by the dark-skinned seamen!

Dingle Harbour has been reduced somewhat since the 1960s. Back then, the north shoreline east from Milltown Bridge ran beside the main road as far as the boatyard and from there along the Tracks (where the train tracks were laid) to Hudson's Bridge. The sea came right up to the street at the western end of the town. The pier had an upper slipway which adjoined the main road and, in southerly storms with high tides, large boats were often deposited on the roadside.

On a platform in the Tracks, where a warehouse stood before it was carried in a storm (years prior to my existence), we played regularly, ignorant of the industry of the narrow-gauge railway which ran the Tralee-Dingle route. Evidence of the railway, which ceased operation in the mid-1950s, was to be seen in the tracks that remained in the ground, running to the pier where boxes of fish were collected for transport to far-off places. The railway station on the Mail Road also had remnants of the rail activity which lasted for more than sixty years.

In 1980, on a visit to America, I came across the engine which had operated the Dingle-Tralee route for several decades before I was born in a museum in Bellows Falls, Vermont. The same engine was repatriated to Tralee in 1989 when a short heritage railway line operated from Blennerville for tourists.

· ● ·

The post office was in Strand Street, across the road from Paddy Bawn's pub (whose owner played football for Kerry and was the most famous person in Dingle at the time). We grew up with the Bawn children and it was in their house that many of us first watched television, in the time of *Skippy* and *Champion, the Wonder Horse*.

While walking home west along the street, a clock was visible high on the wall inside the post office window. The light inside the post office would be left switched on until around eleven o'clock and this was how we knew the time going home at night when clocks were scarce. On the same street, Danny Flahive had a shop that carried miscellaneous gifts, figurines and assorted holy pictures. Danny's brother Tommy transported fish from the boats in a horse and cart. He was also the town undertaker and kept a fine, ornate horse-drawn hearse.

Smith's corner in the Holy Ground was a meeting point where some of our gang stopped for a while before heading to the nearby O'Connor's shop where fruit ices were served. O'Connor's had the first jukebox in the town and it became a popular hangout for teenagers in the 1960s. We would congregate there; the long-haired boys dressed in bell-bottom trousers and flowery shirts with rounded collars, in the midst of mini-skirted girls. We would pose before going dancing in the Phoenix Ballroom in nearby Dygate Lane.

In the summer evenings, we would spill out into the street in our finery and engage in the conversational thrust and parry of the young. Romances were imagined, and some founded, while we drank lemonade and listened to the latest songs by the Beatles and Elvis. It was the dawning of the showband era in Ireland and the emergence of the Flower Power era in America. Young people were starting to have fun. The bands that came to play at the dances in the Phoenix included The Vanguard Six and The Kerry Blues.

At the weekends, when the boarded cinema floor was taken up to reveal the maple dance floor, budding Fred Astaires danced to the music of Chubby Checker and Bill

Haley. At the start of a dancing set, all the boys would be on the east-side wall eyeing up the talent as the girls lined up on the west quarter across the empty middle. As soon as the music started, a swathe of eager, testosterone-filled hopefuls crossed the divide to try their luck and work their charms. The Cronesberrys, a local middle-aged brother and sister, gave displays of jiving in the middle of the floor. Patrick (Cronesberry, son of the town crier) would throw Mary Ellen over his shoulders and her bloomers could clearly be seen under her billowing skirt by the audience who had retired to the balcony for refreshments.

· • ·

The cinema was a prized asset and provided a welcome route of escape from daily life where John Wayne, Audie Murphy and numerous Hollywood stars entertained us at day's end. The monthly film poster listed the upcoming films and left us in eager anticipation of the treats to come. I see now that any small town that had a cinema in those days was lucky in a way I didn't realise back then. The films transported us to other worlds and allowed us to get lost in the make-believe of the Silver Screen. Tom Coffey, an ardent cowboy fan, would run along Dygate Lane after a showing of a Western, slapping his rump while singing, 'To the dump, to the dump, to the dump, dump, dump' – a colloquial version of the 'William Tell Overture' which featured in several Western soundtracks at the time.

We also learned about the world at large through the travelogues which played before the main event. Pathé

News was instructive to our small-town minds about the political goings-on in the world, though what we learned was mostly long after the fact. The film came in reels and sometimes the projectionist would play the second reel first. This would lead to vigorous foot slapping on the boarded floor as a protest to the befuddlement of our brains. At other times, the same commotion would ensue when the foresaid projectionist would sneak out to the nearest pub, Jack Neddy's, for a pint and return too late to change the reels.

We would stock up on sweets as finances allowed before the film. There would be much rumbling in pockets for secreted treats while the film played and it was ritualistic to keep a favourite morsel for the main event. This led to a still much-used quip in our house when someone keeps things for later – 'Save it for the big film'. One of our gang was particularly stingy and used a well-practised movement of drawing his hand under his nose as if clearing it to conceal the fact that a sweet was being deposited in his mouth, lest anyone ask him to share. He was once described as having the wherewithal to peel an orange in his pocket.

• • •

Located next to O'Keeffe's corner, Nell's was another popular fruit ice stop where a long bench inside the door accommodated half a dozen chatterers. The old lady, Nell, was proud of her colourful fruit ice creations and liked the company of young people. After long years of closure, Nell's is again an ice cream emporium, now selling 'designer' ice cream. At the corner, Strand Street turned north into Green Street, which had a bank, the Catholic church, and the Presentation Convent. It also had a water spout from a well pouring onto the footpath. Two of the houses had crests in the plasterwork which were a leftover from the days of the Spanish Armada. A solicitor, auctioneer, doctor and dentist lived on the street, as well as a great character called Katie Sarah, who always looked cross but wasn't.

Green Street had the first chip shop in town. It was owned by the Murphy family whose head, Tipp, was a well-known character. This place also became a hangout after the cinema for banter and to get a little more out of the day. The T-junction at the top of Green Street gave on to Main Street where we spent a sizeable part of our youth in the Temperance Hall. The footsteps traversed from our house to the Hall by various members of the family are innumerable.

On Sundays after Mass, a crowd gathered outside the Hall and the adjacent pub, Peggy Ashe's, waiting variously for the pub and the Temperance Hall to open at twelve o'clock. This audience had a clear view of the Mass leavers approaching from the church, and commentary on the fashion of the day and the latest morsels of local gossip were bandied about, along with English soccer results and the latest Gaelic football news. It could be a daunting passage, turning the corner in the face of this band of experts and, in some cases, ne'er-do-wells.

The location beside the Hall – the Canon's Corner – served as a gathering point for young men from the higher end of town. In my younger years, the Teddy Boys culture arrived, and small groups who had adopted that mode of dress would meet at the junction. One such aficionado added a sinister element to the culture; he would start sharpening a penknife on a windowsill and point it in the direction of school-age children (me included) as they turned the corner. It was probably misguided, harmless fun by the young man in question, but proved scary to those on the receiving end.

Goat Street was uphill from the Temperance Hall. For a while in the 1990s, it became known as Upper Main Street by yuppie types but is now, thankfully, restored to its rightful title. A large stone, the Holy Stone, lies at one side of the street. This curious spectacle that the street seems to have been built around, which is supposed to be a leftover from the march of rock and ice during the Ice Age, now takes up two fine parking spaces.

Further along, Goat Street turns into Ashmount Terrace, and the old hospital is lodged at the juncture of the two. This end of town has a high elevation and housed mainly fishermen and their families who were relocated from the lower Colony. We would access Ashmount on the way to Cnoc an Cairn (a hill overlooking the town from the north) through the fields from our house. The Green, a large pasture to the south of the Terrace, provided another shortcut which was well-worn by fishermen going from the Quay to the Terrace at dawn and dusk.

Three elderly sisters lived in a big, imposing house on the Green. Michael worked there in his early teens as a houseboy and minder of children who were a little younger than himself. He would also do the shopping, which included buying cigarettes and newspapers for the well-educated trio. A descendant from that house, Dr Hilda Moriarty, inspired 'Raglan Road', the famous poem by Patrick Kavanagh. She was also the muse for several other poems by Kavanagh who became enthralled with her when he observed her passing along Raglan Road in Dublin on the way to university when she was a medical student.

The Green was a vast playground for us Quay boys and our theatre of war where opposing gangs pitted their wits against each other, brandishing bamboo spears and arrows. It was in the Green where a gang of us first feasted on cigarettes (Boston was a famous brand of the time) which one of our number procured from their parents' shop.

•••

Downhill, on Main Street, people were richer. Two banks, a hotel and several merchant shops were part of the financial artery that kept the town ticking over. The Protestant church was located in the middle of all this commerce. The Ashe family, who acted as the area's Guinness agent, lived on this street and, in the 1970s, they hosted their Hollywood cousin, Gregory Peck. As our great-grandmother Elizabeth was also an Ashe, our father claimed that we, too, were related to the famous actor who won an Oscar for his role in *To Kill a Mockingbird*.

Curiously, Peck and our father were the same age and had the same birthday. When our Uncle Jeremiah, a well-read and intelligent man, was told that he might be related to Gregory Peck, he responded, 'I don't want anything to do with that Hollywood divorcee'; a statement which reflected the Catholic mores of the time.

Maud's was halfway down Main Street. This was a pub we frequented in the days when we first got a taste for alcohol. Maud was a pleasant lady and had two lovely nieces of our age who visited each summer and worked behind the bar. Their annual sojourn in Dingle greatly enhanced the attraction of the pub.

The Spa Road branches off at the bottom of Main Street at the Small Bridge. This road carried us to the creamery before Christmas to pluck turkeys and, in later years, to the Western Ballroom, which opened in 1969 and became the main dancing venue in the town, heralding the end of thirty years of dancing in the Phoenix Ballroom.

The fair day's buying and selling was held at what was once a brewery site, across from Fred's pub, where many a bargain was agreed upon. During the weekdays, the road from the creamery would have a long queue of horses and carts lined up, carrying milk tanks. As the farmers waited their turn to deposit their produce, they would engage in discussion on topics common to their livelihood and the general state of affairs. Like many such gatherings of people from the rural hinterland, the visit to the creamery was a social event which allowed human exchange for many people who lived in isolated places.

· • ·

John Street goes uphill from the bridge, and Barrack Height, a narrow walkway which one entered at the Mall, exited on this street. Barrack Height was a much-travelled thoroughfare as it was the access point to the side entrance to the Christian Brothers School (CBS). Many scuffles went down outside the school gates after class and assignations of a more romantic nature occurred in the dark seclusion of the Height after dances in the cinema.

The Mall is a long and wide street. Our only reason for traversing its wide passage was to get to the CBS, whose manicured gardens and stepped walkway were kept for the Brothers alone; the plebeian horde had to make do with the Barrack Height entrance which split the courthouse from the Brothers.

Years later, Barret's pub, which was run by Madge and named 'The Club' by our circle, gave us a far more agreeable reason to visit the Mall. Madge was a great character with a good sense of humour and a hearty laugh. She ran a welcoming house beneath the low ceilings of her domain. Joining the Mall and Dygate Lane was Pookies' Lane (lane of the fairies), a small, dark laneway where only brave couples attempted private assignations. At night, the sound of the Mall River flowing nearby added creepiness to the quiet atmosphere of the lane.

· • ·

The Dingle Skellig Hotel is built on the site of the old coastguard building at Emlagh. The red-bricked building, which once housed eleven coastguard workers' families, was a ruin when we played there in the 1960s. The rocket house was situated on the shore side of the coastguard building. Practice was held on the site by the coast-watching service. The members would gather and simulate a rescue by tying a line, with a breeches buoy attached, to a high pole, and hauling a member along its length. The rocket house stored the equipment for carrying out the rescue of seamen from ships at peril on the coastline. This included a horse and cart for transporting the accoutrements to a cliff side. In those days, a rocket with a line attached would be fired from the shore onto the deck of a ship. A subsequent – stronger – line would then be hauled from ship to shore to carry out the rescue. My Uncle Jeremiah was part of that service.

The old Dingle corn mill (mostly a ruin in the 1960s) at Milltown operated as a timber mill; the mechanism of the mill which was traditionally operated by the mill wheel was utilised and converted to electric power. The sawmill, where roofs were cut and all manner of moulded timber sections were run off, served as a valuable resource for local joiners and builders. The old railway station on the Mail Road, now a funeral parlour, ceased operation in the mid-1950s. The station in our time provided for exploration and served as a playground until we were chased off. Because of our desire for diversion, we were constantly being chased away from land and buildings where we trespassed. At the back of SuperValu in Holy Ground stood the remnants of another old mill, known as McKenna's, another hangout used frequently by the lads from the Quay.

· • ·

Gypsy horse-drawn caravans would periodically be seen in the streets. Travelling families, bronzed from the outdoors, would arrive in their colourful carts and homes and add a carnival atmosphere for the duration of their stay. Their entourage would include fortune tellers and numerous colourful characters. The annual Dingle Races would draw a similar troupe which included jugglers, penny-pick and roulette operators. Card tricksters and Jack-in-the-box performers vied for their square footage on the field in Baile an tSagairt.

All manner of local characters added their own form of enterprise to the day of the races. One year, a courageous local Jack-in-the-box paid dearly for his enterprise when a devious player threw a block of wood at his head instead of the customary rubber ball. The race commentator had a unique grasp of English grammar and was noted for his hilarious announcements over the loudspeaker.

In the 1950s and 1960s, annual entertainment centred around the Dingle Races and the Dingle Regatta, with both events held in August. These mass gatherings introduced a holiday atmosphere and working people took their holidays to coincide with the convivial goings-on. The races were held midweek, on Wednesday and Thursday, and the regatta took place on Sunday. At the time, the races were the big event of the year. They offered two days of sport, carnival and entrepreneurship, mixed with songs and storytelling at day's end in the huge tent on the field where porter was thrown back with abandon.

Another tent would have meat pies and sandwiches for sale to the hungry horde. One year, the Thursday card was postponed due to heavy rain until the following Friday and the committee got a dispensation from the presbytery to sell meat pies on the traditional day of fast. The merriment continued late into the night in town when punters returned to celebrate their winnings and drown their sorrows.

· • ·

The Dingle Regatta celebrated the maritime heritage of the town and allowed hardy fishermen show off their prowess at rowing, as well as highlighting their endurance and stamina. The racing was taken seriously by the competitors who would spend evenings at practice weeks before the August day. One boat race, consisting of twelve oarsmen and a coxswain in a seine boat – a long, sleek-hulled vessel that was used for deploying nets for seine fishing – covered a long and arduous harbour course which had the men falling breathlessly over their oars on completion. The seine boat race included visiting crews from the coastline of the southern Iveragh Peninsula. All of the boats, needless to say, were of wooden construction at the time.

The punts – smaller hulls which were used as tenders by trawler owners who kept their larger boats at moorings in the harbour – were raced by crews of two oarsmen. This event, which would have a dozen or more boats involved, had a particularly local flavour, as it pitted pairs of rivals who normally worked beside one another, in the fishing industry.

Single sculling races in the punts were also a feature of the regattas. Sculling is done with a single oar which pivots on the transom of the boat and trails over the stern into the water. The sculling skill involves moving the oar laterally while rotating it at the same time, clockwise and anti-clockwise alternately, so that a forward thrust is achieved. Not all were proficient in this skill which was hard to learn and demanded some innate instruction from the brain. Strangely, the best sculler of boats at the time was a man who was deemed to be less endowed with ordinary skills of comprehension.

Canvass currachs (*naomhógs*) were also raced, with crews mainly from the western and northern parts of the Dingle Peninsula, as well as from Galway and Connemara. The regatta races were held on a course which ran parallel with the shorefront. Throngs of spectators lined the street and had full view of the boats and the finish line. The pier would also be chock-a-block with people of all age groups soaking in the atmosphere and, in those days, the oft-present sunshine. The pubs along the Quay had their biggest day of the year, dispensing Guinness between the individual races and long into the evening. Singing and yarn-spinning went on into the night.

The regatta was mainly organised by leading fishermen and boatyard workers. As one of the latter group, I was shanghaied to help with the advance advertising and fundraising for the event. Regatta dances were held to raise funds in the lead-up. In 1970, the singer, Dana, was booked weeks prior to her Eurovision win with 'All Kinds of Everything' to perform at one of the regatta fund-raisers. She performed in the Phoenix Ballroom to a packed house on the night after her triumph in Amsterdam – a considerable coup for the organisers.

Dingle Boatyard social in Benner's Hotel. Dingle, early 1970.
Seated front, author. Extreme right, Boatyard manager, John Regan.
Included: Elizabeth Regan, Peter and Mary Leonard, Finbarr Callaghan,
Jack Neddy O'Connor, Paddy Barrett, Joe Babs Flaherty, Barney
Birmingham, Jerry Begley, Jack Shea, John Hanafin, Leo Brosnan, Laurence
Courtney, Tommy McCarthy, Paudie Sugrue, Eddie Leahy, Seán Fitzgerald,
Ciarán Regan,

Angela O'Connor and P. J. O'Dowd wedding. **L to R**: Anthony, Carmel, Joan, Mary,
P. J., Michael, Angela, Michael snr, Ignatius, Nuala, John, Bernadette, Ambrose.

John O'Connor, 1966.

Four brothers, late 1960s, in the backyard of 122 The Wood.
Ignatius, Ambrose, Michael, Anthony. (photo taken by John O'Connor).

Mary and Nuala in The Wood, early 1960s

John O'Connor, 1972.

Nuala in Lisdoonvarna, 1966

Mary and Nuala, Lisdoonvarna, 1966.

Michael and Joan O'Connor with American visitor,
late 1960s.

L to R: Michael O'Connor, Joan O'Connor, Vis., Michael, Ambrose,
uncle Jeremiah O'Connor, John, Anthony, Ignatius. Late 1960s.

Daredevil John O'Connor on top of wall, 1970.

L to R: Patrick Curran, neighbour from The Wood; Nuala, Michael O'Connor, Michael jnr., auntie Eileen O'Connor, Mary, Angela.

Nuala O'Connor with Nicky Hawes (future husband) in The Wood.

John O'Connor beside the Favourite -
boat built in Dingle Boatyard, 1970.

Michael and Joan O'Connor with grand-daughter Orla O'Dowd.

Michael O'Connor with grand-children Orla and Deirdre O'Dowd
- with wellies1970.

L to R: Bernadette, Michael,
Joan, Ambrose, Michael snr.,
Ignatius - all O'Connor

L to R: John, Michael and Ambrose O'Connor - with P. J. O'Dowd.

Carmel O'Connor, Elizabeth Graham, Margaret McKenna,
Angela Fox, Ann Long - in the Mall, Dingle.

Pioneer gathering in Dingle. Joan O'Connor, 2nd from right, seated.

THREE

Poverty

·· ● ··

The cloud of poverty loomed large over our lives; it was the one constant that hung there like a January sky, which often touched the ground and lingered languorously before rising again. The hunger, the cold in winter, the lack of appropriate clothing, and the social stigma were symptoms of the condition that had to be endured, with no foreseeable end in sight.

While growing up, the frustration of my parents grew in tandem with the expanding family. Providing food and clothing on a daily basis and clean napkins for the newest babies were just some of the head-wrecking tasks facing our mother. The vexatiousness and frustration brought about by shortages in the household budget which rippled out from our parents around the house are understandable in hindsight but, at the time, were incomprehensible to us as children.

We could not understand why our mother was cross and tormented at times and why our father had to leave the house after supper to do night work unloading lorries. The requirement for our father to find extra work after his postman rounds was fulfilled the best he could, and with enthusiasm, but the extra work was not always there. Fortunately, there was a postman's wage coming in each week and that kept us from extreme destitution.

In Dingle in the 1950s and 1960s, poverty showed its sad face in several streets. The Quay area where we lived had a number of laneways where indigent fishermen's families lived. The Garraí (where my father came from), the Colony, Ashmount Terrace, parts of John Street and Goat Street, all housed numerous people where income was sporadic. Richer people, mainly business owners, lived in the town centre, while some rich farmer/merchants lived on the good land in estates on the periphery of the town. That was the main geographic spread of the people.

While we all shared the same streets, cohabiting civilly, we all knew our place. If we, the poor, were seen loitering too long outside a shop or big house we would soon be asked to move along. 'What are you doing here?' would be the stern rebuke or 'Get back to the Quay where you belong'. On a daily basis, you would be left in no doubt as to your station in life.

· • ·

Historically and universally, the poor have been treated as outcasts; nuisances to be pushed to the outer rim of society. Their plight is ignored by many and is seen by others as a self-imposed condition, acquiesced to without question by ill-educated people. I, however, would ask who would rather be sated than hungry? What child would not want warm clothing and good shoes in winter? The epithetic descriptions of the poor range from the unkind to the downright insulting: the less well-off, low-income families, layabouts, the great unwashed; Les Miserables.

Being helplessly ensconced in the bosom of poverty is bewildering and can often leave one feeling worthless in the face of one's fellow man. Children were bullied at school by both fellow students and teachers because they were poor. Often, strangely, you could be put down by one of your own, too. I used to wear a rust-coloured jacket which was given to me by my father. It was stylish, for the times, and was a good fit for me as I had developed into a broad-shouldered, if lanky, teenager. One whom I considered a good friend, and who came from the same social background as me, commented on the jacket in a put-downish sort of way, pointing out that it belonged to my father.

For some reason, that stung to the point where, on finding a photo at home in which my father was wearing it, I coloured the jacket over with blue pen to make it look different. My insecurity of self, because I couldn't afford my own clothes, drove me to that silly act of defacement. Now, when I see that rust colour, it takes me back to the jacket and the feelings I had about it. Long before the jacket incident, when I was six and going to the convent school, my attire put the incident of the jacket in the shade. If our mother didn't have enough pairs of pants, she would slit a skirt up the middle and re-sew it to resemble a short pair of pants; I cannot remember getting grief over that ensemble.

· • ·

Next to the insulting sideswipes about dress and deportment, hunger was the worst. We were lucky in that, at the back of our house, we had the strand where periwinkles and cockles were plentiful. In the summertime, we would raid gardens for gooseberries and apples, not alone for the adventure, but to quell the hunger. After one such incursion into private property, I was reported to the owner, having been seen by a rival picker. He later accosted me in the street and administered a full-palm whack in my face. I remember my sister Angela and I picking up discarded apple cores (we called them stumps) from the street, dusting them off and devouring any remnants of remaining fruit.

When I was in my pre-teens, I fainted a number of times due to under-nourishment. One day, I was standing at the front door with my mother when I collapsed. A passing neighbour advised my mother to take me in as the air was too strong for me. My sister Nuala, after coming home from school, was told by my mother that I was dead. Mom loved a bit of drama; it was a distraction from the trying times she went through.

· • ·

Joan did her best, though. On returning to the house in the evening, the smell of her freshly baked bread was heavenly. This mostly occurred in the early days of the week when a few bob from the previous payday still remained. When she began baking a loaf with the dough spread out on the red formica-topped table, I could hardly wait to taste the fruits of her labour. The tantalising odour wafting through the house was a joy. In later years, Joan's pot roasts were another treat. That came about because the oven of the gas cooker had failed and all cooking had to be done on the hob.

At table, our mother would put the margarine on our bread lest we overdo it and waste any. If eggs were on the menu, they would be distributed in halves to members of the hungry horde who had to wait their turn for the spoons. If anyone brought home extra money following some enterprise, a full egg was given out when circumstances allowed. Goody – a mix of warm milk, raisins and bread – was a treat that was often served up as a main course. Jam jars would be used in place of cups, while saucers and side plates were an unknown concept.

If one member was favoured over another during the distribution of the meal, there would be kicking under the table in protest at the perceived injustice. When I had started earning a steady wage at Dingle Boatyard, I would occasionally be rewarded with a dessert – most likely Ambrosia Creamed Rice. This motivated dissention in Mary who once exclaimed, 'Dessert for one and none for the other, I'm sick of this shit'.

When peeling spuds before boiling, one would be castigated for taking too much of the potato away with the skins. When they were cooked in their skins and on the table, our mother would do the peeling and distribution.

All endeavours where wasting food might occur were overseen scrupulously by Joan. In the midst of our poverty and want, there were good times. We may have been famished for five days, but we feasted for two. We were skinny but not completely ragged.

· ● ·

Clothes were passed down naturally and an old photo of the twelve of us, taken in the 1960s by a person unknown and which came to light when we were all adults, shows us reasonably rigged out. I don't know how our mother managed it. The clothes for the boys would start with me and work their way down through all the brothers. By the time they got to Ambrose, the youngest, their sell-by-date was truly expired. Mary's wardrobe would end with Bernadette, the youngest girl. Our father did temporary repairs on our shoes to keep our soles from scraping the ground. In summertime, we would happily go about barefoot.

I cannot remember owning a toothbrush or seeing toothpaste in the house at any time; it's a wonder how we now have teeth in our mouths! There was very little we could call our own, and even if we did have any possessions, we had nowhere to keep them. There were no personal lockers and very few hideaways in a four-roomed house with twelve people vying for space. After the number of people in the house thinned out, Bernadette got a locker and thought it was a precious thing; at last, a place in the house to call her own.

In the bedroom, the window boards of the wide stone walls acted as shelves for our comics. *The Dandy* and *The Beano* vied for space with *The Topper*, which was my favourite. Later on, the boys, having found a desire for longer adventure stories, found entertainment in the illustrated sixty-four-page reads which featured war and Wild West stories. These treasured volumes were regularly swapped with friends and classmates.

· • ·

The St Vincent de Paul would call to us at Christmas with a hamper containing the staple requirements, including a box of biscuits in a USA tin which looked square in dimension but whose lid only fitted one way. This almost square-shaped box was a geometric mystery to me at the time but the contents were a feast and evidence that Christmas had arrived.

Our father would get tips at Christmas from his postman rounds and arrive home on Christmas Eve with a trove of coins, and singing 'O, You Beautiful Doll' if he was tipsy. He would deposit them on the kitchen table where our mother would do the 'divvy up'. We would each get a shilling or sixpenny piece, depending on the generosity of the haul. Sometimes Dad came home with the gift of a goose from a farmer on his postman's route.

One of my memories of Christmas Day is waking up in a freezing cold house. This overshadowed any joy I got from the presents our parents had managed to produce in spite of all the other necessities required amidst the expectations that exist at that time of year. As the day wore on, the fire heated the place and our hunger was sated by the Christmas meal. To some extent, an atmosphere of merriment prevailed and this well-being was reinforced by the thoughts of the Wrenboys on December 26th and the chance to make a bit of money collecting for the Wren (or the 'Wran', as it is pronounced).

The tradition of the Wrenboys, who went 'hunting for the wren' on St Stephen's Day is ancient and was practised throughout the country. Dingle is one of the few remaining towns where the tradition is still alive. In my great-grandfather's time, the first group of Wrenboys to arrive at Lord Ventry's estate on Stephen's morning received a £5 note.

For us, Wren's Day was an opportunity to add to the house coffers by collecting money. Our group of 'smallies' would entertain the neighbouring houses, playing a toy drum and tin whistle whilst singing 'Jingle Bells' and other Christmas ditties. On Christmas night, there would be frenetic searching for old colourful garments and pillowcases to fashion into 'rigs' (outfits) for the coming day. Our father played the fife and tin whistle and had an assured position as a musician in one of the bigger Wrenboys groups.

• • •

In general, there were people in the town who were good to us. Although the shop on our own street gave us nothing, the Ashe sisters' shop in the Quay was good for a bit of tick (goods without payment until the end of the week), as were as a couple of shops further over the town. Greaney's and Sheehy's grocery shops were good to our house. Nuala was often sent for the tick; her personality was deemed the most suitable for begging. We even got our hair cut on tick. It was a case of 'My mother will pay you next week' to Danny the barber when the hair was already on the floor.

Lots of people got tick in those days and I'm sure that the shop owners were exasperated by the continuous trail of people in want coming to their doors with large gaps between remuneration. After our Mom died, I found out that a kind bank official had given her loans, though meagre, to help with the bills.

Towards the end of the 1960s, our Mom got word that she had been left some money by a distant relative who'd died in England. There was joyous anticipation after the registered letter arrived from a solicitor. The weeks went by with an air of expectancy prevailing and much talk of how the money would be spent. We, finally, saw hope of deliverance from the penny-ha'penny place we were in. On the strength of the promise of riches to come, our mother incurred more than the usual debt with shops in the town. When the legacy finally arrived, it was modest – enough to live high for a very brief period only. We all got a small share from the money and our mother, as was usual, spent very little on herself.

· • ·

The 'penny man', an agent for a furniture shop in Tralee, would call to the house weekly looking for money for items of furniture my mother would have bought on HP (hire purchase). HP was used by all low to middle-income families then, and only the barest necessities for running a house would be purchased; buying a comfortable armchair would be considered a luxury. The penny man had a pointy, bald head and he once told me that I had a lovely head of curls.

When my mother was broke, she would often go out to the backyard when the penny man was due, ordering us to answer the door and tell him that she was not at home. This was a job we all tried to dodge and squabbles would always ensue; it was a case of 'I did it last time' and 'No, I did it last time'.

My father was frugal and would always manage to have a small amount tucked away in his handkerchief. It would be coins mostly; he would try to save enough of them to buy a pack of Gold Flake cigarettes. In the early years of our youth, our father took a drink, no more or no less than many working men, but the realisation came when the family was young that there was no money for drink in the budget. In later years, when some of the children had gone from the house, our father would give some of his cache to our mother so she could go to Bingo – her only escape from her worries and troubles.

Once my parents started having children, their dancing days were truly over. There was no money to spare for the cinema or any other activity that incurred payment while a house full of children needed food and clothing. They had to wait until ten of us had grown up to socialise together again, and that was at family weddings and baptisms.

· • ·

Nowadays, eating fish is considered chic and the right thing to do, but fish reminds me of our poverty. We ate potatoes and fish a lot. My father would be allocated a plot where he sat spuds, as we called them, and he frequently got fish from the boats when the weather suited. Boiled whiting was a dish we were all familiar with – it looked miserable and tasteless to most of us but we had no choice only to eat it.

If the potatoes were finished up for the year, we would get a slice of bread to soak up the watery soup from the plate. Until the end of his life, my father remained a lover of boiled fish and its soup, which was flavoured with pepper, whereas many in our family hardly give it a second glance now as we saw too much of it.

Nowadays, I sometimes observe the mollycoddling of young kids at table. They don't want different foods touching on their plate and show an instant dislike for foods they haven't even tasted. I see some mothers cooking perhaps three different dinners for their children. I tell them to cop on and give them a dose of poverty from time to time.

· • ·

Throughout the town there were degrees of want in many homes. Some homes with smaller families, where a

49

reasonable wage was coming in, also had nothing to spare at the end of the week. But for those on the breadline, the shared embarrassment of poverty was evident in the interaction with like peers; we were like co-conspirators in a plot. We ended up together in the cheap seats, as it were. Other than for the purposes of tourism, a rich man's son would seldom be seen on the pier when the boats were landing their catch. The Quay boys were there to cadge a bit of fish to sell or to bring home for our supper. We smelled of fish, as we were often told when assuming a position above our station.

The people living in the countryside on small holdings were somewhat better off than the townies because of their vegetable produce and fowl that assured them of more constant meals. That said, many of them didn't have much advantage in other areas – they dressed like us and carried themselves with a similar air of dejection.

. • .

Memories of poverty stay with you forever. The frugality practised out of necessity in the past stays with us and will ring alarm bells in the present to remind us of the cost of things, even if we are now in a position to buy anything we want. Our father had a thing about turning off the lights after we got the electricity installed. There would be war if a light was seen lighting during the day. In his later years, Dad was still watching the amount of coal he would have on the fire lest it ran out too soon.

Our mother would borrow a clothes iron from one of the neighbours on a regular basis. In later times, some of us still borrowed things until it struck home that we could now afford our own clothes iron or food mixer, or whatever. It was ingrained in us from an early age that we would never have those things; that they were beyond our remit as poor people. I see it in several of my siblings; their attention to cost saving is a throwback to the leaner times of old.

Like a visible scar on one's skin from an accident when young, poverty leaves reminders in our psyche which come back to haunt us, even in our well-positioned adulthood. However, it is not so much the deep hunger or the hand-me-down clothing we remember, it is the way we were treated – like a different caste – by people who were, luckily for them, better off.

Tommy McGovern **left** and Michael O'Connor, in Dingle Bay.

Boys in the Temperance Hall.
Michael O'Connor, 2nd from right.

L-r: Michael O'Connor, Carmel, Joan, Anthony, John and Angela O'Connor

Carmel and Ignatius O'Connor

Bernadette

Nuala

Wedding of Bernadette and Richard Underhill, **seated centre**, with
Michael and Joan O'Connor - in Benner's Hotel, Dingle, 1977.
Includes brothers and sisters, and grand-children of Michael and Joan.
Parents of Richard: Doris and Ozzie; **back, 2nd** and **3rd from left.**

Mary Danaher with son Michael. Lisdoonvarna, 1971.

Dingle Boatyard, late 1960s.

St. Colette on sea trials in Dingle Harbour.

Storm in Dingle 1948.

The Gas Shed. **L to R**: Martin Flannery, Paddy 'Ollie' Brosnan,
Jimmy Kennedy - husband of author's aunt Liz O'Connor Kennedy.

Michael O'Connor, centre, at Dingle Regatta, 1970.

The Tracks in Dingle - where the Dingle-Tralee train ran until the mid-fifties.
On the left a Nobby fishing boat is hauled up in the newly- opened Boatyard.

Eask Tower on Carhoo hill with (inset) coast-watching hut.

Local youths in a punt east of Dingle pier.

Michael O'Connor's **Fórsaí Cosanta** medal which he received in 1945
following his service in the Coast-watching service.

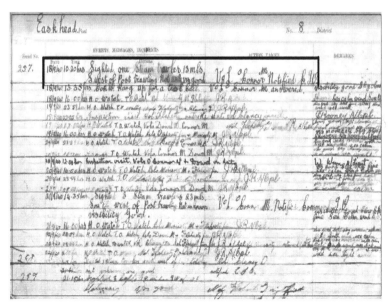

Page from Carhoo Hill look-out post log-book, dated September 1940.
A highlighted notation shows an entry by *Volunteer O'Connor M* (author's father),

Chart of the hamlet of Reenbeg on the south side of Dingle harbour
where the author's great-grand-mother, Elizabeth Ashe, came from.

The ten O'Connor siblings at a family gathering in 2014 outside their home.
Inset are childhood images of each person.
L to R: Carmel, Bernadette, Anthony, Michael, John, Ignatius, Mary, Nuala, Angela, Ambrose.

FOUR

Schooling

·•··

In recent times, I saw a man remove his rumpled hat and pause reverentially as he passed the gates of the Christian Brothers School in Dingle, and I thought what a misguided, foolish and unfortunate individual he was. I wondered if it was possible that he hadn't had access to a newspaper or a radio in the previous twenty years. I was in awe of the man's gesture – which was a throwback to a much earlier time – as well as being deeply moved by the apparent sincerity of the action. Then anger set in and my lips moved as I uttered the words, 'That shower of hypocrites'. Even from the grave, they still had a hold over the weak.

The man had the look of a rural dweller as he walked peculiarly close to the buildings along the street, almost brushing against them. He was on the far side of middle age, humble in demeanour, and carrying a thin tree branch as a stick as he dragged on the last quarter of a cigarette. I had an absurd urge to approach the septuagenarian and seek out the reason for his obedience to the Brothers who had once resided beyond the gates which sported black crosses on the pillars.

The exalted edifice inside the pillars once housed the local congregation of the Brothers who purported to follow the ideals of Edmond Ignatius Rice, a man who gave succour to the poor and marginalised and who founded the Order to further those ends. But the benevolent ideals of the Kilkenny man, dating from the early 1800s, got lost along the way. In place of the plan to educate and bring along the less well-off, in particular, was a new set of rules which gave favour to the banker's son and which drove the poor further into the mire, emotionally and physically.

The tall man with the stick must never have seen the physical and emotional abuse meted out to unfortunates whose make-up and standing in the town fell short of the guidelines in the newly corrupted rule book of the Christian Brothers. The reverential man with the squashed hat must never have seen what I had seen within the Gothic-windowed building on the lofty perch above the street.

I had watched several times while one of the robed ones sexually abused a classmate in front of the whole class. As a punishment, the white-haired offender, seated, would have the student stand in front of him with arms outstretched while he tickled the boy's upper body before moving his hands down and inside the boy's trousers. The session of abuse would go on for more than fifteen minutes while the mortified student looked blankly into the distance. This abuse was not a one-off occurrence; that same student – a 'favourite' – had to face that ordeal several times during his time in that Brother's classroom.

I cannot recall now what was going through my mind as I witnessed the terrible sight of that young boy being mercilessly degraded and used as a plaything in front of his peers by one who was supposedly closer to God than we were. And further, I will never imagine what was going through the boy's mind, but I do know that his later life was much troubled.

Another, the Superior of the bunch, would at every opportunity let the less responsive students know how useless they were. If a correct answer to a question was not forthcoming, his sneering remark – delivered in the most sarcastic manner to those of us who lived around the Quay – was, 'Ye'll get a job fishing anyway'. He was the first truly insulting man I met; he made me and my neighbours feel like we were just taking up space; that we were lost causes. I spent a year with the two I have referred to, and together they succeeded in stifling any interest I had in learning, and degraded, each by their own means, the human dignity of several of their charges.

Another Brother, whom I encountered in primary class and whose relatives hailed from my own town, would leap for maximum effect – like one would take a good run at a physical chore – as the half-inch thick leather strap came down on a child's hand. Another favourite weapon of abuse by this tall Brother, who was big and strong, was a chunky portion of a sash bar, like that found on a window. That man epitomised how the cloak of power could be used for evil intent and how pent-up frustration spilled forth on innocent unfortunates.

The punishment meted out by the Brothers – with their precisely-dimensioned purpose-made instrument of torture, the black strap – was totally disproportionate to any wrongdoing; and not knowing the answer to 'something' was considered a wrongdoing. Consider hitting somebody today because they didn't answer a question correctly. And while acknowledging that rambunctiousness by some 'hard chaws' had to be addressed to maintain classroom discipline, some Brothers were just plain cruel. Those times at the CBS were more like being in a punishment institution where the boys went home in the evenings.

To be fair, another Brother I encountered in my junior years was not the worst, and that is the best I could say about him. He once humorously remarked that he could wallpaper his room with all the sick notes I brought to school from my mother. It was in his class that I heard of the assassination of John F. Kennedy.

There were also lay teachers in the CBS and they largely turned a blind eye to, if not condoned, the cruel regime in which they operated. Their attitude to the Quay boys was pretty much that they were a bothersome inconvenience to the natural flow of their Latin and algebra lessons.

The Christian Brothers have a lot to answer for. Their infractions against the human body and the spirit of young men are numerous, but perhaps their most egregious sin is the way they stifled the pursuit of learning in many of their students. School was a humiliation to be faced each weekday and the Christian Brothers, the biggest bullies of all, beat us with what appeared to be a relishing fervour.

I was fortunate, however, and managed to rise above the labelling, the belittling and the emotional scarring visited on me by unkind men with sad lives; men who got their kicks from further weakening the weak. I know many who were turned off forever from the classroom by these men in black. These were boys who never got the chance to experience the world of learning and, moreover, of learning freely without fear of prejudice or mockery while in that pursuit.

· • ·

The nuns in the Presentation Convent, where my siblings and I were first introduced to learning, were marginally ahead of the CBS when it came to showing compassion to their charges. They, too, had their *grá* for the rich people's children, though one of them, Sr Kevin, did encourage me to pursue music lessons when she saw I had a leaning in that direction. They did provide a much looked-forward-to breakfast on the day of First Holy Communion.

In retrospect, I realise they had their own frustrations. One in particular, who treated all students the same, exhibited a constant torment which her pupils bore the brunt of. There was a non-teaching nun, Sr Bernard, who worked in the kitchen, and she would occasionally take me from the play yard to the refectory for a bite of food during lunchtime. Her name was synonymous with the famous dog found roaming the wilderness with a small keg of nutritional liquid strapped round his neck for forlorn strays.

At fourteen, I went to the Technical School, or Tech, as it was known, and started learning in earnest. There I encountered more boys like me who were disenchanted with the CBS. We were all treated the same in the Tech if we showed any interest at all in the subjects on offer there. But learning is a two-way thing and you had to meet the educators halfway. Some of the students were just passing time and behaved in an unruly manner, which was stamped down forcefully by the headmaster.

I was a model student, apparently, and found my niche in technical subjects. The rural science teacher (Jerry Hussey) gave me the responsibility of measuring the daily fall of rainwater and entering it in a logbook. In the space of a couple of months, I came a long way from the belittling sarcasm meted out by the so-called educators in the Mall. My sister Mary also attended the Tech and excelled in the learning environment there.

· • ·

In the beginning, we had no books or pencils to speak of; none of the accoutrements of the classroom would be found on our person. We had to suffer the embarrassment of sitting beside one of the richer children and reading from their pages. In some cases, the cruelty of children would come into play and they would remind us of our station with remarks like, 'I don't want to sit near him'. I guess they feared they would catch some unmentionable disease, like poverty.

Some days, as we walked over the road, we kept looking back to see if our mother would beckon us home again, something she did on occasion when she saw the reluctance in our demeanour, and took pity on us. Our father never condoned our being kept home from school and we would hide when he came home for his eleven o'clock break. We were often caught out and our mother would bear the brunt of the telling-off.

On weekday mornings, the radio had sponsored programmes that we would listen to while in bed upstairs. They were in quarter-hour slots and each had a signature tune which became familiar over time: *Buy Lyons tea, the quality tea, drink Lyons tea, Lyons the quality tea* was the Friday morning jingle, and we delighted in that one as it heralded the last day of school for another week.

Then there was the school yard where the usual scraps played out, alongside more sinister exchanges. A banker's son, who had a brutish demeanour, would kick me in the bare shins several days of the week and await my response. If I had told my mother of the assault, she would have marched into the bank and confronted the father in full view of all; she always stood up for her children.

A misfortunate family whose house backed onto Barrack Height beside the CBS grounds had trying times from several school bullies. The father, who had an unfortunate nickname, was strange, and the son, who attended the CBS, was quiet and introverted, a ready victim for bullying by unkind youths. There was a lean-to tin shed at the back of their house which would be pelted with stones to draw the father into a confrontation. The treatment meted out by school-goers to the father, who often interceded on behalf of his child, and to his son was horrible and often sustained mercilessly. The mother of that persecuted family was a midwife who attended at my delivery into the world. I look back with compassion at the sorry goings-on. I witnessed the distasteful side of unthinking youngsters who never considered what if it was their family being tormented.

• • •

There was £10 a year available to households where the Irish language was spoken. An inspector would call to conduct an oral test and those in the house that were attending school would be lined up before him. My father would be at work and my mother, who needed the money more than any other mother in the neighbourhood, stayed in the background lest she was asked to speak in Irish. She silently prayed for a positive performance from the ones sitting in the hot seat.

It was like the Spanish Inquisition, with emotional rather than physical torture. A waiting period for the result of the test was filled with hope and anticipation of the respite from hunger the money would bring. However, we never qualified and the much-needed subvention to the household purse was not forthcoming. The experience sowed sour seeds of distaste associated with the language that persists to this day for me and some of my siblings.

Generally, for people living in town, English was, and still is, the first language, and schoolchildren who didn't even have books for school had little hope of learning much of anything, let alone a second language. In later years, I saw another side to the speaking of the Irish language reflected in the symbol of the *fáinne* – a gold ring worn on the lapel by *Gaeilgeoirs* who would seldom suffer the ignorance of those without the ring. It reflected a form of elitism that can still be found in some circles. There was also possessiveness about the spoken Irish exhibited by some fluent speakers who would correct the townie when he or she was trying their best. I have a good command of the language now but am still reluctant to use it in the company of those who think they own it.

• •

Schooling of poor children was never meaningfully embraced by the educational institutions of the 1950s and 1960s. One would never hear a well-schooled child saying things like 'I don't want no such a thing' or 'I didn't say nothing'. The double negative was always a tell-tale sign of a neglected education. It may be observed that in this more enlightened age grammar has improved.

When we went to school, our parents were hopeful that we would be improved by the experience, though they realised the uphill battle we faced amid the prejudices of the day. They knew we were severely disadvantaged by not having the necessary books to help with the process of learning. Schoolbags, pens and copybooks were also basic requirements of the time that we had minimal access to, and there was no packed lunch to give sustenance halfway through the day.

The sketchy and perfunctory schooling on offer to us in Dingle when we were young didn't prevent me or my siblings from learning by other means, or from returning to education in later years. We have all achieved success in various pursuits which required work, training and commitment. The opportunities denied to us during our young school years, due to our economic and social station in life by begrudging educators, in many ways instilled in us a resolve to succeed and to prove that people from the Quay area, whatever their aspirations – be it fishing, teaching or the pursuit of the arts – are capable of coming good.

FIVE

Clergy

·· ● ··

'Get up for Mass! Mrs Landers is gone over.' We would hear the loud call from our father as he rapped the bottom of the stairs with his knuckles while we lay in our beds in the big room on Sunday mornings. At that stage, the time would be creeping up to eleven o'clock – the time of the last Mass of the day. In our bedroom there were no clocks or wristwatches and Mrs Landers, a farmer's wife from the country, as we called it, was our Sunday morning alarm. The saying, 'Mrs Landers is gone over', is still used within our family when we are about to be late for something. We would have heard the clip-clop of the pony as it approached from the west but we purposefully and mischievously waited for the arrival of the horse and trap outside our house before making a move to alight from the bed.

Our father was a pious man and demanded that all under his roof attend Mass. Our mother's chief concern as she faced the mirror while we trundled down the stairs was that her headscarf was straight at the back before she walked over the street. We went to Mass because we had to and, in later years, chiefly to maintain peace in the house. Some of us would pretend we were going to Mass but would go walkabout until it ended, making sure for later interrogation that we found out which priest had been on duty.

Mass was not high on my list of priorities back then and, in retrospect, I partly understand why. Along with the patrons – many of whom were sincere – in the top seats of the church, were hypocritical personages who kowtowed to the clergy and gave little heed to the people in the back rows.

The Corpus Christi procession through the town in June was a spectacle which publicly highlighted the control the clergy had over us. All the men walked together, marshalled in straight lines by 'holy' stewards who would hardly talk to a poor man the following day. The women were similarly toeing the line under instruction from members of the Legion of Mary. Girls of First Holy Communion age would scatter flower petals from a basket before the processional Host. If baskets were scarce due to the numbers of young girls participating, those available were given out by the nuns to the children from the 'right side of town' first. This was an indignity suffered by the girls from our house.

All of the houses along the route of the procession would have holy statues in the windows. These proclaimed more kinship to the men who lived in the presbytery rather than devotion to the Host being transported under an embroidered canopy which was held aloft by selected acolytes. I cannot recall anyone from my neighbourhood, nor any of my relatives, ever getting their hands on the gold-painted poles which held the canopy aloft. During the procession, hymns such as 'How Great Thou Art' would be sung as pseudo-pious people sang beside families who were in want of food and clothing. When I hear those hymns now, I think of our subservience to false people when we knew no better.

· • ·

The clergy were apart from the people they ruled over. Yet, we were not absorbed by this; it was a fact of life at the time. In our house, the rosary was said every night after supper and all present had to participate. Pictures of Pope Pius XI and Pope Pius XII were on the walls of our house, and in every home in the neighbourhood, as was the ever-illuminated Sacred Heart picture which hung over the fireplace. The rituals of the Lenten fast (eating fish on Friday) and going to Mass on Ash Wednesday (when ash is rubbed on the forehead) were, and still are with the older set, scrupulously, and willingly in many cases, adhered to. However, many who followed these rituals found the exhortation to 'Love thy neighbour' a big ask.

It is from the modern perspective that those days in the 1950s and 1960s are seen for what they were, and the true social climate of the time is revealed. We were under the thumb of the Church and its Orders of priests,

Brothers and nuns and, to some degree, the sycophants who bowed to those Orders; the unordained ilk whose patronage allowed the Church to prosper authoritatively and financially. There was a time when the priest in the pulpit would call out the list of donors for the 'Stations' (a twice-yearly Church calendar event) and the amounts given. One can imagine the cowering of the humiliated poor people present, whose contributions were in pennies.

· • ·

The Holy Mission came to town and the missioners preached fire and damnation instead of bringing bread and compassion. The robes of these messengers were brown, setting them apart as a higher form of apostle from the usual bearers of the 'message'. The stalls outside the church sold beads and pictures of the haloed heads of saintly men and women whose messages and true beliefs had long been twisted into a tool to keep the ordinary people down. Religion was used as a device to scare and to keep certain people in their place lest they become enlightened about how the world really worked.

In most houses, including ours, there were special cups and saucers which were kept for nuns and priests when they visited. Ours was a China set which had been given to Michael and Joan on their wedding day. None of us, to this day, ever drank out of the rose-painted Delph; jam jars were the order of the day for drinking around our table.

The awe in which the clergy was held is understandable. Its members represented our religion – our beliefs, our faith, and the rules by which we lived. And while many were ambivalent about their devotion, there were genuine followers who saw through some of the 'makey-up' aspects of doctrine and practised according to true Christian beliefs and teachings. These devout members are the ones who were badly let down by the clergy.

It is evident now that many vocations were suspect and it is commonly known that families forced their children into the service of the Church; a Church which deemed that women lacked purity after childbirth and had to be reintegrated into society after a period of seclusion; and that unbaptised innocents went to a made-up place called Limbo. Then there is Purgatory, where I no doubt will languish interminably following this heresy. Historically, cardinals, fortified with ample food and wine, made rules for the proletariat to live by, rules that were often far removed from Christian and humanitarian teaching.

For a long time, they were successful in maintaining their hold over the weak-willed in every town in Ireland. Then, long before the turn of the century in which they prospered, their world started to collapse and their influence started to wane. Church scandals became the order of the day and the men in black began to walk with their heads down.

• • •

In the late 1960s, at least in Dingle, a more approachable and seemingly accessible type of priest started to emerge, a priest who was there for all the community. At that time, one such priest became one of my best friends. Father Lawrence Kelly was involved with the local Temperance Hall where I had a position of responsibility. He and I managed the running of the club at the Hall, and the man's humanity was without question. He taught me to drive in 1970 and regularly gave me the loan of his car (a green Opel Kadett) to drive members of the club to the Killarney picture house as a treat for the voluntary work that we did.

Following Fr Kelly's transfer to another parish, Fr Fleming arrived on the scene. He showed a similar interest in the club and continued his predecessor's perks to members – his car was a Vauxhall Viva. In later years, another man of the cloth became a sailing companion and a close friend, proving again that there were exceptions to the rule. Also, to be fair, there were others among the ordained who had their hearts in the right place. That handful, however, was normally in the background and had no power to change the system which sheltered those religious colleagues whose Christian values were suspect.

· ● ·

In more recent times, as the less-well-off started to find their feet – a change brought about by the changing times and children who came good and made their parents proud – the clergy have had to show more respect for the wider congregation. People who had, hitherto, been close-mouthed and lacking in confidence began to speak up for themselves and creep out from under the influence of the white collar. Disenchantment with the Church has come home to roost and, as I write, parishes in Kerry and further afield are finding it difficult to have Sunday Masses in their churches due to lack of priests.

Society has taken a new and more modern direction, which may be too far off track for some but we are at its mercy because the once-admired and relied-on, steadying influence – the Church – abused its power and privilege and eventually lost the respect of the people. The recollections I put on paper here will no doubt offend many of the devout, and, while it is not my intent to offend those genuine people of faith, I'm sure that some, especially those who lived in Ireland in the times mentioned, will be sympathetic to my view.

SIX

Work

· · ● · ·

During the Second World War, when my father was in his mid-twenties, he got a job with An Fórsaí Cosanta (Defence Forces). He was stationed for the duration of the war in a hut beside Eask Tower on Carhoo Hill, a location which gave a wide view over Dingle Bay and its coastline. Eighty-three of these lookout posts (LOPs) – Eask was post thirty-six – were manned around the coast by the Defence Forces. Coast watchers had responsibility for identifying and reporting aircraft and shipping movements as well as monitoring communications between ship and shore.

My father, Michael, would cycle round the harbour past Burnham to the base of the hill before climbing the steep slope to the top where the tower stood beside a mass-concrete hut constructed to house the coast watchers. He would stay for a number of days at the lofty lookout point until relieved. There were twelve coast watchers sharing the shifts. A notable and recurring entry in the ledger for the lookout from the time refers to my father: *Volunteer O'Connor M., returning from Mass at 1000hrs.*

After the war years, on receipt of a positive report from his commander, my father took up employment as a postman. He did his delivery rounds on a bicycle and his route brought him a couple of miles into the countryside. After supper, he would frequently upend the bike on the kitchen floor in order to mend punctures and do repairs to the brakes and mud guards. The bicycle was his vehicle for carrying out his job and there was no allowance for the wear and tear of his mode of transport. The hiss of pumping tyres would signal the completion of the repairs and the bike would be ready again for cycling on the bothereens of the hinterland of Dingle town.

Dad's uniform and greatcoat were always clean and in good order. When the greatcoat was replaced by his employer – the Department of Posts and Telegraphs – the silver buttons with the embossed harp were removed from the old one and the coat was recommissioned as a blanket for one of our beds. When the fish were going, our father got evening work in the local fish-processing factory (a co-operative run by the fisherman and known as the 'Scheme') gutting and filleting fish – cold work in wintertime.

• • •

From a young age, the boys in the house delivered newspapers and sold them outside the church after Mass. We all had our own customers and war would ensue if another tried to muscle in and steal someone else's customer. My brother Michael unloaded coal from steamers when he was scarcely sixteen. Local merchant, landowner and entrepreneur, Michael O'Sullivan, provided employment for several people from the Quay neighbourhood and beyond. My sister Angela worked in his private house for a number of years while I worked on the O'Sullivan farm, saving hay in the summertime and tending cows and pigs throughout the year.

At a young age, one of my jobs was driving a sow from the farm through the streets to visit the boar at the far end of town – a job which elicited wise cracks and coarse banter from the gauntlet of yahoos needing entertainment along the way. I delivered milk in the evenings with my sister Mary on a horse and cart. We would tackle Dolly, the horse, to the cart after school and load up with crates of glass-bottled pasteurised milk. Dolly was a timid horse who quickly got used to the new man in her life.

There appeared to be an expectant air about Dolly's stable at four o'clock in the evening when I arrived to don her tackle and hitch up to the wooden cart. After loading up was done, we set off on our rounds and, like the horse in the film, *The Quiet Man,* who stopped abruptly outside the pub, Dolly had a similar intuition and would slow down and halt outside her customers' houses. Hordes of children would cadge a ride on the back of the cart as I drove through the town. Ignatius also worked on a farm and became the second milkman in the family.

· • ·

Any monies accrued from our collective enterprises would be handed over at home, though some of us had private endeavours going on. Ignatius claims he had the first ATM in Dingle – a secret hideaway in a stone wall a couple of hundred yards from home. He would deposit a fraction of his wages here lest he be left with nothing if he brought the whole lot home. Angela was the only one who knew his PIN number – she knew which stone to remove! Every conceivable secret nook at home where one could stash a little something for their own entertainment had long been discovered.

I would break up wooden fish boxes (for firewood) for a woman who owned a pub on the Quay; she also rewarded for the collection of empty glass bottles. For my labours I would get a glass of raspberry cordial and a stale bun. An elderly lady, Hannah, who lived in the Garraí, regularly gave me a thruppenny bit for a bundle of sticks. We would do everything we could to stave off the hunger and, once that was taken care of for another day, our thoughts would turn to the cinema and the joy of having fifteen pennies (one shilling and threepence) to distract us for a while from the drudgery of a skimpy life.

All of my family, except my mother, picked periwinkles at some stage, not for our own consumption but to sell to a local merchant, Michael O'Sullivan, so our mother could buy bread, milk and margarine. Our father would get fish from his fishermen pals when the boats landed. On the strength of our father's name, we would cadge a strap of fish from the boats as they landed the catch and sell it to Timmy, who had a fish shop in an adjacent laneway.

A dentist's house in Green Street employed half of our family at various stages. My mother, along with my sisters Nuala, Angela and Bernadette worked in the dentist's house as domestic workers; our father did painting jobs and a bit of gardening there while I, after I had acquired some manual skills, did small jobs and hung wallpaper.

We all sought work and found it in order to sustain our own needs and those of the wider household. Our father worked in the evenings and on Saturdays unloading lorries, cutting grass, painting, and undertaking any job he could to add to the house purse. At night, when the household responsibilities were taken care of for another day, our mother would go working for a few hours, doing office cleaning and, in the 1960s, doing kitchen work in the newly opened Skellig Hotel.

There were a number of employers who were good for giving weekend and holiday jobs. The Ashes, who were the area's Guinness agent, gave out summer work to students washing bottles. They bottled their own lemonade and orange drink and also supplied Nash's very popular fizzy orange. Several of the town schoolboys who attended the CBS in the Mall found work directly across the street for the summer holidays. Plucking turkeys in the creamery in the run-up to Christmas was another good earner, as was selling race cards on the days of the Dingle Races.

· • ·

In 1966, the year I finished my second-level education, I worked for a local vet during the summer holidays. My task was to keep a record of the farms visited and of the cattle that were tested for bovine brucellosis. I spent eight weeks travelling around the peninsula with Tadhg, the vet, and Joe, who came along to do the heavy work of keeping the animals placated while being examined. It was my first extended taste of the countryside. Joe was good fun and liked to get one over on this townie whenever he could. Many cups of tea were drunk in farmhouses around the peninsula during the operation.

In January of the following year, 1967, I began my boatbuilding apprenticeship at Dingle Boatyard; I was in full-time employment for the first time. Apprenticeships lasted five years and the wages were incremental on a yearly basis. After twenty years of my parents living in The Wood, my wage became the second steady income coming into our home. I remained in the boatyard for six and a half years. Mary and Nuala left home around this time, leaving an emptiness behind, after finding work in a hotel in Lisdoonvarna in County Clare. It was the beginning of the thinning out of the household.

My brother Michael started salmon fishing during the summers of his late teens. He got a rounded transition from youth to adulthood in the company of the colourful characters in the fishing fraternity. He took to the sea with a casual ease, like his ancestors before him. Michael and I were the two from the family who inherited the salt in our veins from our paternal ancestors. Ignatius left home at a young age and lived in the Harrington household as a residential farm boy for a number of years before emigrating to London. Anthony moved to Lisdoonvarna for work, and Ambrose, after completing a carpentry apprenticeship took the boat, as they say, to England.

· • ·

The boatyard experience was the foundation for my learning and branching out into other endeavours. It was where I not only learned my trade but also where I transitioned from childhood to adulthood. Several apprentices of my age group were taken on at that time and it was the norm for each new apprentice to be placed under the guidance of a qualified shipwright. I was lucky to be placed with a skilled man who filled me in quickly on the politics of the boatyard environment. As with all newcomers, I had to put up with the antics of some senior members – these included being sent on several fool's errands during my first couple of weeks at the boatyard.

Some of the established tradesmen were secretive about their craft and reluctant to pass it on to youngsters, while others were forthcoming and delighted to impart their knowledge. At the time, I was not fully aware that I was becoming part of a noble and highly skilled trade in the company of exceptional craftsmen. In later years, I became involved with other woodwork trades but they did not compare in skill and intricacy to the craft of wooden boatbuilding.

SEVEN

Play

·· ● ··

My childhood images are mainly of the environs of the harbour. From the upstairs landing window of our house, we saw the harbour each morning. The tower of Eask on Carhoo Hill over Burnham stood like a sentinel overlooking the sheltered waters to the north and the expansive sea of Dingle Bay to the south. The iconic image of the stone edifice, with its wooden hand pointing east to the harbour's mouth, will be stamped in my mind forever. It was always there, immovable, a witness since 1847 to the maritime heritage of my ancestors. Moorings on the harbour below held fast the fishing fleet wherein the boats, with majestic names like the *Angelus Bell*, *Madonna* and *Majestic*, pointed to the wind and tide.

On Good Friday, the boats would dry out on their sides for their annual painting, close to the shore in Strand Street. The paint was supplied by Mikie Long, local fount of knowledge regarding all thinks marine, from a building close to the pier which functioned mainly as a pub, thereby giving valid reason to the fishermen for several visits during the black day (pubs in Ireland remained closed on Good Friday) for a top-up of paint. Long before I knew the working of the tides, I was fascinated by the sight of the large sea-going vessels lying on their sides, scattered randomly like beached whales on the sandy shore by the Quay. The workings of nature were being used to deposit the fleet for this spectacular occurrence during the equinoctial tides.

It didn't suit us when the fishing boats were ashore by the pier as it curbed one of our seagoing adventures – it meant the punts (wooden rowing boats used by the fishermen to come ashore after mooring their larger boats) were moored off and out of reach. Family and friends would 'borrow' the punts when they were ashore by the slipway, mainly on Sundays, for our own adventurous jaunts around the harbour. Anyone who had a set of dowel (thole) pins, which acted as fulcrums on the gunwale of the boat for the oars, was in luck, as the rowing could not be done without them. The owners turned a blind eye to this activity once there was no horsing around and the boats and their crews were returned safely at the end of the day.

We would row to the idyllic southwestern corner of the harbour where Lord Ventry had set up his mansion. The building was then owned and run by an Order of nuns as a private girls' boarding school. It was like another world inside the walled gardens of Coláiste Íde (as it was, and still is, known). The grounds were lush with tropical vegetation including bamboo, which was prolific. We would cut the bamboo and fashion it into spears and arrows for our forays into the hills in pursuit of cowboys and Indians.

On Sundays, the nuns would march their giddy charges along the two-mile trek into the town to attend a play in the local school or other such event that was deemed suitable for the brains and manners of the young girls. The marching troupe of over one hundred girls would pass the Cottages. Their dark garb consisted of black stockings and shoes and the shepherding nuns also wore black from top to bottom. The moving swathe of black inevitably got a moniker – the Black Pollys – from the local youths. Unbeknownst to Ignatius at the time, he would one day marry one of these girls after meeting her in London, far from the shores of Dingle Harbour. His wife, Mairéad, also came from a large family and hailed from the island of Oileán Chléire, off the southwest coast of Ireland.

Rafts constructed of waste wood and logs were another means by which we got on the harbour; we would propel the raft using a long pole like those used by Venetian gondoliers. The rafts were put together without finesse and were ungainly looking, as well as being unsafe. A severe telling-off from our parents would be visited upon us if they got wind of our rafting exploits or, indeed, of any activity that brought us near the sea.

Many of us could not swim until later in life due to being constantly warned off water-based activities. The sea was seen as a necessary means for fishermen to make a living but not as a plaything for the trifling pursuits of youngsters who didn't know what they were doing. Yet, we defied the advice of our elders as young people do and lived adventurously as close to the edge as possible – pushing out the boat, literally and metaphorically.

· • ·

The tower on the hill would be visited when adventures close to home got over-familiar and a diversion from the ordinary was called for. It was a considerable hike from the town around the periphery of the harbour before the climb to the summit was tackled. On reaching the top, the view over the bay is spectacular but that meant little to us at the time; when people are hungry for food and distraction, the value of scenery is far in the background of their consciousness.

There is a hut beside the tower which housed my father and his fellow coast watchers in pairs during the years of WW2. The roof was gone from it by the time I and my family members frequented the place, and only a semblance of the accommodation remained. We didn't realise at the time that our father had spent the war years in that hut, but when I climb the hill now it is foremost in my mind that I am retracing the footsteps of my father who would spend five days a week, for more than five years, in the confined space of the cast-concrete quarters. The remnants of a fireplace and a rusted bunk bed were also visible. Window openings, long bereft of glass, looked out to the bay and graffiti had found its way to the ghostly lookout, six hundred feet above sea level.

We would walk east from the tower along the ridge of the hill to see the harbour's entrance below us, and stand on the ground where the hamlet of Reenbeg once stood. We were again ignorant of our family history, this time of the fact that our great-grandmother Elizabeth Ashe came from that place. We know nothing when we are young.

Across the way from the hill at this point is Slaudeen, a small beach near Hussey's Folly (another iconic image from Dingle). This was the boys' beach in summertime and the 'Banks' – another extended beach – stretched west along the shore from here. This was our Costa del Dingle where we would languish under the sun and play in the clear water without a care, apart from the embarrassment of our whiteness at the beginning of the season. While walking home in the evenings, the sense of a day well spent was overshadowed by the uncertainty of the week to come.

· • ·

Cnoc an Cairn (hill of stones), which we saw in the distance to the north of our house, was good for another Sunday adventure. Before going to the top, we would explore the quarries at the bottom for treasure as these had become a dumping ground for various items of junk. The quarries were originally formed when clay and stones were dug up to act as ballast for ships (steamers) returning to their ports from the harbour. On the way to the top, we would burn the furze with wire-handled canisters that contained compressed rags soaked in paraffin. This is now a controlled activity but when it is allowed and the smoke wafts over the town, the smell from the burning hill always brings with it the memory of those times.

There was a small tower of stones at the top of the hill that always seemed in need of repair and we would all lend a hand at topping it up until the next time. Cnoc an Cairn joined with the 'stony' hill which extended to the north and provided for more extensive exploration. After I started working, one of the first things I owned was a transistor radio, and my sister Bernadette and I would take to the hill on the evenings to listen to Radio Luxemburg.

Close to our house there was a stepped white wall which prevented the sea coming onto the road at high tide and we would congregate here in summer with our neighbour friends. We looked for flat stones on the strand to have competitions at skimming in the harbour, a game in which the girls participated with equal gusto. For a time there was a fad, which Carmel enjoyed, for communicating with cans tied to the end of a long string; an imitation of the telephone which had made its way to Dingle in the 1950s.

The girls and their pals played shop; they made make-believe ice cream blocks from wet sand and dished it out between slate fragments acting as wafers. Pádraig Lynch, who hailed from the tailor's house, taught the girls how to sew and embroider. The Slatterys and some of the Sheehy family also used the white wall as a gathering place when the weather was fine. The strand was stony and seaweed abounded, but that didn't stop us from wading in the water. Mary once got a serious gash – needing stitches – from a broken bottle. It was the first time I saw a profuse amount of blood spilling from a wound.

We were mostly barefoot in summer and the soles of our feet were hardened like leather. In the evenings, we would go home bronzed from the sun once the early days of burning were over. After one hot day when I got severe sunburn on my naked back, Michael drew a hairbrush along my red skin as I lay in bed in agony. Sometime later, when I had recovered, he was paid back in full when I jammed his head in the backyard gate.

While at play, we were removed from the otherwise humdrum nature of our days, but the downside of exhaustive physical activity during the day was the concomitant increase in hunger that went with it; a hunger which would not always be sated at day's end.

• • •

Street games were popular with boys and girls. Marbles, with their glassy swirling colours, were a great attraction for a time. 'Knuckling down' and flicking the glass sphere which nestled between thumb and forefinger brought anticipation of winning more of the prized 'taws' – a term which was generally used by us. Rounders was played like American baseball, but without the bat. A rubber handball was hopped on the spot in front of the player who would, in turn, palm it away forcefully into the distance. Runners would try to retrieve it before a circuit of the course was completed by the spot player. Handball was a very popular street game which we played against the ice plant wall and off a large gable beside the creamery. Motor cars were few and far between at the time and interruptions to the game were minimal.

My sister Mary participated in every game she could get into; she was known as the tomboy of the family and, to this day, is an ardent follower of all sports, especially Gaelic football and the Manchester United soccer team. Mary was not one for the hula hoop, an imported twirling plaything for girls which was in vogue in the early 1960s.

Football would also be played in the street and in open spaces around the pier. The balls were in short supply and normally owned by well-off and spoiled children who would sometimes cease to participate and take their ball home if things were not going their way. Gaelic football was played in Páirc an Aghasaigh, and apart from the organised and competitive side of the game, we would gather after school to pick random teams and kick about for an hour to fill the gap until supper time. Soccer would also be played in the GAA grounds, in contravention of the then sacrosanct ethos of the field. Of the boys in the house, Michael was the most accomplished footballer and went on to win several medals at competition level.

One activity which, in retrospect, sounds silly was that of running alongside a bicycle wheel rim that had been denuded of spokes and was propelled by a piece of stick; we called the wheels 'bowlies'. When people from the countryside came to town to go to the cinema or a concert, they would leave their bicycles lying behind a building in the Tracks (a stretch where the Dingle to Tralee train used run). We would borrow the bikes while the film was playing, mostly on bright summer evenings, and go for a cycle. If our parents caught us or got wind of our exploits with other people's property, there would be war, and several times we would round a corner only to find our mother or father smack in front of us.

• • •

Stray donkeys were often commandeered by the Quay boys and kept in secret places until the owners turned up to take them back. Riding around on the back of a donkey, we emulated scenes from films we'd seen at the cinema, like that of John Wayne on horseback in *The Searchers*. The influence of the cinema and the Westerns was large in our life. In the game of bang-fall-out, which we played in the fields and gardens with crooked branches in place of Colt pistols, we imitated the derring-do of heroes from *Gunfight at the OK Corral* and *The Alamo*, where Davy Crocket met his fate. My first introduction to the heroic frontiersman was in a school play when I was seven and played Davy in a Christmas play. My entry from stage left, singing, 'Davy, Davy Crockett, king of the wild frontier' is still vivid in my memory. For Christmas that year, I got a silvery plastic gun and holster which was complemented with a black imitation felt hat.

Run-away-knock was a favourite game but a damnable inconvenience for the victims. On the way home at night, we would knock on doors and run like hell along the street. There were a few clients who gave a good chase. The more they let us know of their annoyance, the more we tormented them on following nights. We were mean, I suppose, but what was the use if a good chase by a beet-red-faced adversary didn't ensue? On several occasions, a member of the group who would be chatting casually on the walk would, without forewarning, knock on a door and scarper before the rest of us had time to comprehend that the game was afoot. A cousin who was using crutches following an accident bore the brunt of an offended house owner's ire while the rest of us were more than two hundred yards away. In Dygate Lane and Grey's Lane, we would get the best value out of the game; the more docile neighbourhoods were not on our list.

· ● ·

Sometimes a game would lose its allure and participants would wander off to seek adventure by other means. I had an episode with a tractor when I was thirteen. Tractors were relatively new to farming in those days and farmers would park them in the town while shopping and having a drink. One day, a friend and I started tinkering with a tractor which was parked to the rear of the Tracks. I still cannot remember how I started the vehicle but as soon as that happened, my friend took off, leaving me to cope with the consequences.

The gear stick and foot pedals had no meaning for me and the tractor started moving jerkily towards the sea wall.

My mind was assailed by two terrifying images – being drowned after becoming trapped in the tractor, and being flayed alive by my mother. In situations like these, it was our mother we feared. The front wheels mounted and traversed the wall to the other side, and the undercarriage ground into the concrete capping on top, leaving the machine and me swaying precariously while the engine continued to roar. I delicately stepped down onto the wall and, looking around, I concluded that the incident had gone unnoticed.

It took a number of days for my fear to abate and for me to come to terms with the foolishness of my deed. Then the knock came to the door. I was lucky, in the main, as the owner of the dangling tractor, which had been restored relatively undamaged, was a friend of my father. Our Dad would admonish us severely before cooling down and moving on to the next crisis.

Inside our neighbour Edwin's wall were wild saplings from which our mother would break a branch and denude it of leaves before fashioning it into a cane. We often got the cane across the back of our legs when we stepped over the line. If we were staying out too late, she would walk over the town with the stick hidden under her coat to herd us home. She had no compunction about administering discipline in public. I am sure that we were a handful for Michael and Joan, but we never caused them lasting grief.

• • •

We played largely with friends from around the Quay who were from the same social class. I cannot recall how rich people's children played or passed the time, but I remember their reluctance to be seen with the likes of me and my sort. I did, at one point, get a reputation for being a bit of a tearaway. I used to climb trees competitively to the highest possible point with like-minded adventurers who wanted to go higher. I would be seen atop tall, deserted buildings and standing on my head on top of high walls and the like. These shenanigans and the story about the tractor didn't help my assimilation into the company of more discerning circles. Indeed, I remember one girl of my age from a well-off family who used to run away when she saw me coming.

I got a lot of bad press, too, for being the leader of the Quay gang (a much vied-for position) in the days when we had competitive street clashes in the Green with the John Street boys, who were always worthy opponents. We engaged in battles in the Green using tree branches and spears fashioned from bamboos. We sought out trees with springy wood to make long bows and searched for suitable y-crooks on branches to make catapults – adding rubber strips from old tyre tubes in order to launch our missiles. A well-made catapult could be a lethal weapon. We mainly used them for shooting at cans and bottles but there were one or two dangerous players who had more sinister intent. One, who was older than the rest of the group, fitted sharpened nail ends to the tips of his bamboo arrows.

For a time, I jumped ship from my Quay cronies and spent a phase in Dick Mack's yard in Green Street. Ronald and Oliver from the McDonnell family were in my class in school and we seemed to hit it off. The family had a farm with milking cows and I used to give a hand after school in the evenings feeding the animals and cleaning the cow house. There was also farm machinery about the yard which intrigued and stirred a want for discovery in me. The adventure was not like work as I enjoyed the activity, and Mrs McDonnell, who always looked busy, was a good woman. She was welcoming and especially hospitable when it came to providing food and lemonade. When the work was done, there was always some other activity to engage with as the McDonnell brothers were inventive and willing to experiment outside the box.

· • ·

We spent our days outdoors in our extended backyard on the shores of Dingle Harbour and beyond. We came home weathered, grazed, skinned and sometimes wounded at day's end. I left a half-crown-shaped lump of skin on a barbed-wire fence while fleeing from an irate orchard owner. Other members of our tribe had their own war wounds which they hid on returning to the house for fear of a backlash. We were chased, cornered and clattered by our peers and, in turn, we chased, cornered and clattered them. If one came home with a black eye, they would be in trouble for hanging around with the wrong sort. A call to our door by a complainant saying, 'Your son broke my window with a stone', or the like, brought the full fury of our parents to bear on us. There was no mollycoddling at home; we took things on the chin and moved on.

In the large garden of a friend, we dug out a rectangle of ground to a depth which allowed us to have a makeshift underground dwelling when the project was roofed with tree branches and 'scraheens' (squares of top grass and earth). It was an imagined hideaway from posses and roaming bandits that might be on our trail. A pipe commandeered from the disused local dumping quarry fed smoke to the outside world from a metal half-barrel which resembled a stove. The ground within the dug-out would be strewn with leaves and dried grass. It was a home away from home where we secreted ourselves and made plans for conquering rival gangs.

In the days leading up to St John's Eve in June, we collected wood, old tyres and other combustibles for the annual bonfire. Doors were knocked on as we sought out items for burning; backyards were trawled through for broken furniture, fish boxes and the like. Each street had its own collection and while we wouldn't normally encroach on the opposing neighbourhoods, having the biggest fire was the aim and, to that end, rules were often broken.

On the night of the fire, periwinkles collected from the strand would be cooked in pea cans filled with water, and potatoes raided from local plots would be roasted on the end of a stick. A gang of boys and girls of all ages would sit around the fire late into the night, gabbing and poking the fire to raise sparks into the midsummer sky. It was only as the last embers faded that we would wander home, red-faced and with our clothes smelling of smoke.

· ● ·

The Temperance Hall, which was part of the historic temperance movement that began in America in the 19th century, played a big part in our young lives. The Halls were traditionally places where young men who aspired to teetotalism would socialise. In our time, it was effectively a youth club for males. The presbytery had control over the Hall and its operations. The transformation of the club from its old-fashioned, male-dominated ethos into the modern age was overseen by the forward thinking and decent Fr Kelly. During his stewardship, I was his right-hand man and looked after the day-to-day running of 'the Hall', as it came to be known.

The Hall had two full-size, state-of-the-art snooker tables – one for the mature players and the second - called the small table even though it was the same size – for the beginners. A long period of apprenticeship was required before graduating to play with the big boys, many of whom had their own cues locked in hanging metal tubes. My brothers Michael and Ambrose were good snooker players and serious contenders at annual tournaments. Michael had to be tactful when playing against Ambrose, however, because the latter, as the youngest sibling, was the pet and news of a thrashing on the snooker table by Michael would not be well received at home.

The production company of *Ryan's Daughter* (made in Dingle in 1969) hired space in several buildings in the town and part of the Temperance Hall was given out for hire. This resulted in a revamp by the film crew. After re-opening, a new arrangement allowed for the introduction of a television and card rooms upstairs, and two table tennis games on a new maple floor downstairs. It was table tennis that attracted the girls to the building and Bernadette was proficient at the game. She took no prisoners when playing with the boys. Most of the girls used the Hall as a hangout where they eyed up the boys, but a handful got actively involved in the other games on offer.

· • ·

In the course of one week during my early teens, I saw both the beginning and end of life for the first time. On the way home through the fields after a trek on the hill, I came across a cow calving, a sight no doubt commonplace to young people living on farms but an exceptional sight for a townie like me. The distress of the animal (as I imagined) and the liquid egress accompanying the newborn was my first introduction to the wonders of nature.

A few days later, as I wandered home along the shore front after a day of adventure around the old coastguard station, which was then dilapidated but still provided ample opportunity for climbing and playing king of the castle, I happened upon an elderly man, whom I recognised, lying on the grass. After summoning help from a nearby house, I found out that he was dead, following a heart attack. I did not have any adverse reaction to finding a dead person on my own at such a young age. I went home and had supper as usual. In those times, there was an acceptance about the ways of life and mollycoddling was not the order of the day.

．●．

In the late 1960s, when some of my siblings and I were working and had a bit of money we could call our own, we would hire a box camera from Walsh's chemist shop on Sundays, rent or borrow bikes and cycle around the west of the peninsula, taking photos along the way (some of the black and white photos from those trips are included in this book). We now live in the digital age and cameras and photos are literally in our faces ad nauseum, but the thrill of picking up the processed film from the shop after waiting for several days for it to be developed kept us excited throughout the week. A camera would also be hired for special occasions like Holy Communion and Confirmation. When I was receiving a steady wage from my apprenticeship, I put enough money aside to buy a projector and had the photos processed as slides. These were a big hit when projected onto a white sheet pinned to the dresser for viewing during family occasions.

An old abandoned railway shed beside the Mail Road acted as a stage where we would enact plays. This pastime was influenced by concerts and plays which would occasionally be held in the town under the management of the nuns or other branch of the clergy, or in the cinema under the auspices of the local dramatic society. *West Side Story* was a film of our time, the first of its kind which showed rebellious youths in the throes of peer and parental conflict. We identified with that and acted it out in our own way. Nothing became of our foray into the world of acting, but our efforts satisfied our want to be individual and to congregate with a purpose for a while.

In my teens, after getting a gift of a guitar and after I had some practice, I got together with three friends, Jimmy, Brian and Seán, and we formed a pop group, The PetSounds. We practised a bit and even had two girls for backing singers. We played at local charity concerts and the like but never hit the big time. That said, it was great fun.

. • .

Muireach, a small village to the west of Dingle, had a famed ballroom where *céilidh* dances were held throughout the summer months. When we came of age, we attended in droves on Saturday nights, seeking entertainment beyond the hills and harbour of Dingle town. *Lá breás*, the girls from the training colleges who had come to learn Irish in the West Kerry Gaeltacht, would be at the *céilidhs* during their sojourn in the area. They were so named because of their familiar salute, *Lá breá* (fine day).

Getting as far as the tin-covered dance hall was usually achieved by means of cadging a lift in some rickety Anglia car. Getting home was largely on foot along the long road (*bóthar fada*) which seemed never-ending at two o'clock in the morning. A key would be left over the door for our arrival home after a late night of carousing. When Michael inquired once, after arriving home in the very early hours, 'Are they all in?', my father fumed: 'Are they all in at four in the morning? Are you daft?' he shouted.

The Rose of Tralee Festival held heats for the Kerry Rose selection in Dingle and in Muireach where a local girl would be chosen to go forward to represent the county. My sister Nuala was chosen from the Muireach hopefuls when she was seventeen and she went on to take part in the West Kerry finals. This happy event brought great pride to our parents and to the house; the wider world was suddenly opening up to our family.

· • ·

The tower on the hill is a lonesome place now, visited mainly by the odd tourist in summer. It's been a long time since a group of children climbed to the top looking for diversion on a Sunday afternoon. Street games are long gone, too, as are the punts and quests for bamboo. Nobody climbs a tree anymore. Corner boys have moved on and the juke box is a now a collector's item. People who visit the house in The Wood ask, as they look out the kitchen window towards the tower, 'What is that up there on the hill?' More say, 'What a view you have from here'. While we were growing up, we took that view for granted. From early morning, it was visible through the landing window and we would see it throughout the day as we played on the shore. At evening, too, when the colours changed, it was behind us as we went inside after getting the most out of the day. Unknown to us, however, and just like the big bedroom, that setting was moulding our character and our essence.

Epilogue

····●····

R eaders who have stayed with this chronicle so far may be interested to know what happened in the lives of the O'Connor family in later years; well, nothing earth-shattering or on a grand scale. In the 1970s, there was still want as no magic box of wealth had opened up so that people could live happy ever after. Everyone had to work hard to attain any semblance of comfort. However, things got better, in general, for the ten siblings in that they were no longer hungry and their wardrobes improved considerably.

The anxieties the O'Connor siblings experienced as children were replaced with a new kind that goes with rearing their own children, who would benefit from the historic challenges of their parents, and their parents' intent to give them a better life than they had. Their parents ensured they had all the accoutrements for early schooling and then provided for them (in still trying times) through college education. The new generation of O'Connor descendants would be winners and would work in education, government, engineering, medicine, hospitality, business and more.

Michael and Joan lived to see several of the new generation and delighted in their potential. They found a measure of enjoyment in their later years attending the weddings and baptisms of the extended tribe. Alas, Joan, who had laboured tirelessly to rear her ten children, died after a short illness when relatively young, and missed out on seeing and enjoying the continuing expansion of her descendants.

In later years, Michael, the father of the clan, began regaling his grown-up children and grandchildren about his years in the hut on the hill by the tower, and telling stories of his youth, when he fished off Iceland. He possessed a peculiar wit which surfaced unexpectedly and often spoke of fanciful times when he lived in a house so big, with a table so long, that the person on the far end was unrecognisable; a wishful fantasy and the antithesis to how his life really was. Michael died six years after Joan passed away.

At family gatherings now, the conversation regularly reverts to the time of our youth and the goings-on in our house in The Wood. And while, at the time, getting through each day was onerous (much more so for our parents than for us children), we see those times now as a place where not only hardship prevailed but also where we acted out a type of communal adventure that still, after many decades, is worth resurrecting.

From my description of the period we grew up in, as outlined in this work, one might be glad to see the back of it and never mention it again, but something else grew out of the strife, something that lasts longer. Each year, in January, the descendants of Michael and Joan O'Connor – the children, grandchildren, great-grandchildren and great great-grandchild – gather to celebrate the life of these much-loved people and to acknowledge their legacy to us.

***

Photo additional to first edition.

Dingle Pier, early fifties.

Michael O'Connor and Joan 'Brennan' O'Connor

Children	Grandchildren	Great-Grandchildren	Great-Great-Grandchildren
Mary	Michael	Helena, Conor, Adam, Charlie	
	James	Chloe, Caitlin, Eoin	
	Caroline	Marie, Katie, Michael	Karlee (child of Marie)
	Adrian	Zack, Max	
	Kyera	Dylan, Darragh, Shauna	
Nuala	Fidelma	Alex, Harry	
	Elizabeth	Laura, Kate	
	Tommy	Matthew, Niall, Ellen	
	Seán	Charlie, Rose, Jude	
	Nicholas	Lea, Sophie	
	Michael	Iarla, Maeve	
John			
Angela	Orla	Robert, Adam, Heather	
	Deirdre		
	Fíona	Christine	
	Aoife	Archie	
	Matthew		
	Michael		
	Patrick	Noah, Fiadh, Blaine	
Michael	Maeve	Amy, Sinéad, Tom, Laoise	
	John Michael		
	Joseph		
	Roisín		
Carmel	Karen	Caitlyn, Daniel	
	Kevin	Kyla, Maddison, Sophia	
	Christopher	Connor, Ellie	
Ignatius	Alana	Jamie, Tadhg, Eoin	
	Nuala		
	Shane		
	Siobhán	Oisín	
Bernadette	John		
Anthony	Caríosa	Daithí, Saidhbh	
	Ruaidhrí		
Ambrose	Stephen	Ava	
	Christopher		

Michael O'Connor and grandson Michael Danaher.

Wedding of Mary O'Connor and Jimmy Danaher, 1969.

Photos additional to first edition.

Married men football team.
Michael O'Connor, second from left back.

*Joan O'Connor and Kathleen Danaher at Mary
0'Connor's wedding, 1969.*

CRAFTSMAN FURNITURE
from a Dingle Workshop

TRADITIONAL AND MODERN
John O'Connor

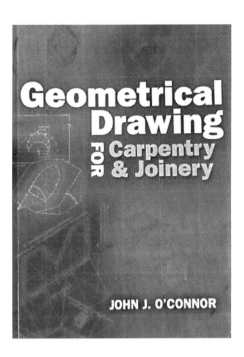

Geometrical Drawing for Carpentry & Joinery

JOHN J. O'CONNOR

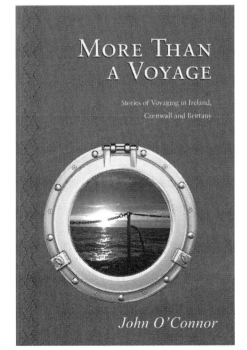

MORE THAN A VOYAGE

Stories of Voyaging in Ireland, Cornwall and Brittany

John O'Connor

John O'Connor is a retired lecturer and a native of Dingle, where he served his apprenticeship to building wooden fishing boats in Dingle Boatyard. He is a keen sailor and a founder of Dingle Sailing Club. John taught students of boat-building, and carpentry and joinery, at the Institute of Technology Tralee for more than 30 years and in 2009 published a college text book, *Geometrical Drawing for Carpentry and Joinery*. John has sailed extensively and published, *More Than a Voyage* which details his many sailing adventures over three decades. He has recently published, *Craftsman Furniture from a Dingle Workshop*, which deals with traditional and modern furniture he has constructed over the years in his Dingle workshop.

THIS EDITION:

Printed in Great Britain
by Amazon